W9-BRB-334

To Joan
from
Mother
1977

REQUIEM

REQUIEM

The Decline
and Demise
of Mayor Daley
and His Era

LEN O'CONNOR

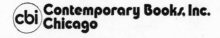

cbi Contemporary Books, Inc.
Chicago

Library of Congress Cataloging in Publication Data

O'Connor, Len.
    Requiem: the decline and demise of Mayor Daley
and his era.

    Includes index.
    1. Daley, Richard J., 1902-1976.   2. Chicago—
Mayors—Biography.   3. Chicago—Politics and government
—1950-   I. Title.
F548.52.D35027   977.3′11′040924   77-75845
ISBN 0-8092-7920-7

Copyright © 1977 by Len O'Connor
All rights reserved.
Published by Contemporary Books, Inc.
180 North Michigan Avenue, Chicago, Illinois 60601
Manufactured in the United States of America
Library of Congress Catalog Card Number: 77-75845
International Standard Book Number: 0-8092-7920-7

Published simultaneously in Canada by
Beaverbooks
953 Dillingham Road
Pickering, Ontario L1W 1Z7
Canada

For Janie,
who has shared the joys
and the burdens

Chapter One

*"I am sorry to inform you and the peo-
ple of Chicago that Mayor Richard J.
Daley is dead."*

—Press Secretary Frank Sullivan

Monday, December 20, 1976, held the promise of being a pleasurable day for Richard J. Daley.

Sunday had been a glorious day for Daley, with his four sons and his three daughters and his thirteen grandchildren gathered under his roof for their traditional pre-Christmas celebration, the doting grandfather holding that his children's children should savor the joys of Christmas Eve in their own homes.

So, feeling contented, the end of the year in sight and with no problems that he was aware of on his horizon, the Mayor was setting forth this Monday on another promising day.

He was feeling as physically fit as any vigorous seventy-four-year-old man could hope to feel, with not a trace of the dizziness and faint chest pains that he had experienced during the previous two weeks. With the media having no cause to snap at him, with the annual wrangle in City Council over his $1.2-billion budget behind him, the Mayor anticipated that he could coast into the new year. With not much more to do than hold court in his City Hall office, he would try to be pleasant in the spirit of the season to even his enemies.

It was Daley's custom at the beginning of Christmas week to

1

host a breakfast for his department heads and others of his official family, the city paying for it out of taxes collected from the hotels and motels. For Daley, a delicious part of the festivity this time was that his devoted wife of forty years, Eleanor (Sis) Daley, had consented to accompany him. Even if you are the greatest mayor that a city has ever had, it is gratifying to have the most important person in your life seated at your side when the people who work for you pay you homage.

The window-peepers of South Lowe Avenue, the Daley neighbors, knew that this Monday was to be some sort of special day when they saw Mrs. Daley, in fashionable fur, come down the walk of the yellow brick bungalow at 3536, reputedly the "nicest house in Bridgeport," and step into the Mayor's limousine. Daley, at her side, and smiling, swung his head in search of faces to be recognized, raising his right forearm a few times, wiggling the fingers of his gloved hand in greeting. He then followed Sis into the car, the limousine driving off, bodyguards in an unmarked black squad car on its tail.

Some sixty or seventy department heads, staff people, and secretaries stood and applauded, about fifteen minutes later, as the Mayor and Mrs. Daley entered a private dining room of the Bismarck Hotel of downtown Chicago. With the ingratiating Colonel Jack Reilly, Daley's one-eyed chief of protocol at their side—Reilly grinning in his evilly benevolent way—the Daleys modestly shook hands with all the guests, the Mayor making an effort to say something personal to most of them.

A silver bowl filled with eggnog was set on a table, soon becoming a pick-me-up place for the guests who had been through the receiving line. A harpist from the Chicago Symphony sat at her instrument, off to one side of the room, softly picking out the notes of familiar Christmas carols and sentimental Irish tunes—the Mayor smiling broadly when she played one of his favorites, "Danny Boy." And then, directed by Colonel Reilly, who announced, "Folks, I think it is time for us to sit down and enjoy our meal," breakfast was served. An excellent breakfast it was: fruits and fresh juices, eggs Benedict, sausage, sweet rolls and coffee, some of the traditionalists asking for *Irish* coffee. Daley ate heartily.

When the tables were cleared, Deputy Mayor Kenneth Sain, hailing from two generations of political antecedents, arose to toast the Mayor and Mrs. Daley, wishing them a happy—"and especially"—a healthy Christmas. Then Sain sat down and Reilly took charge. In his strident Eastern accent the Colonel paid his personal compliments to the host of this feast and to Mrs. Daley. Clearing his throat and cocking his head toward Daley, Reilly then said: "Mr. Mayor, I asked all of these people who are gathered here, 'What do you give to a man who's got everything?' So we put our heads together and decided: a trip to Ireland, where we know you are loved and which you love."

Mayor Daley looked joyful; he turned to Sis and said something privately, and she smiled. On his feet then, accepting an envelope containing airline tickets from Jack Reilly, Daley motioned for Sis to get up and join him, but she shook her head and would have none of it; in all of their married years, even when Daley coaxed her with "Oh, come on, Ma!" she had never allowed herself to be placed in a position of upstaging him. So Daley expressed his thanks, telling his people that they were the great people who were helping to make the great city of Chicago great.

Finally he said, "So from our home to your home, we wish you only one thing—good health, happiness, and a very merry Christmas." As the throng scrambled to their feet, vigorously applauding, His Honor the Mayor, looking now as if he had successfully got through yet another function, headed for the door.

At his desk, having walked over the one block from the Bismarck, Daley riffled through a small number of messages that had come in before his arrival. A banker had called. Mike Bilandic, alderman of Daley's 11th Ward, had called. More important, Bill Lee, president of the Chicago Federation of Labor, had called—to confirm that this was the morning that the Mayor was to meet with him and leaders of the various unions which were getting generous 1977 contracts from the city.

The annual visitation of Bill Lee and his group was not so much a matter of seeking assurances from Daley that the city would continue to pay private-industry rates, as it was a year-end courtesy call, sort of a ceremonial to acknowledge that Daley was labor's man and that Daley knew it. The Mayor, in a fit of temper, might tell a banker like Chairman A. Robert Abboud of the mighty First National Bank to go screw himself, if he pushed too hard on something—but Daley would never lose his cool with the labor chiefs.

Shortly before noon, having zipped through the paper work on his desk, the labor chiefs having been in to pay their year-end respects to Santa Claus, Daley buzzed his secretary to let her know he would be leaving now for his next appointment. A bodyguard was standing at the threshold of his office, holding his coat as he came out. Another bodyguard was already out in the fifth-floor hall, holding an elevator.

On the main floor of City Hall, Daley marched through the corridor to the east side of the building—the Clark Street side; he had vague information that some people were doing sculpture on some blocks of ice, directly below the metal Picasso that dominated the Civic Center Plaza. He would admire the sculpturing for a few moments, expressing holiday greetings to anyone who looked as if this was expected, including any visitors to the city who might have the temerity to approach him, regarding him, as many visitors did, as one of the major sights in Chicago to be seen.

This was Daley's day for sculptors, apparently. Not only had Bill Lee and the other union guys been in to give thanks that they had once again carved out a good deal for their members, Daley had also been visited by a sculptress named Eleanor Root, who presented him with busts of himself and Sis, gushing, "You're the most wonderful and best Mayor in the world!" Losing interest now in the ice sculptures, and perhaps feeling the December cold, Daley had turned to a bodyguard in the Civic Center and said, "Let's go." The bodyguard turned his head, flexed an index finger, and Daley's limousine pulled up to the curbing on the Clark Street side, the tail car behind it. Daley got in and off they went.

This was to be as long a drive from City Hall as the Mayor could have, remaining in the city limits. The Chicago Park District had constructed a $548,000 gymnasium in Mann Park, in

Alderman Edward Vrdolyak's ward, in the southeastern extremity of the city. In accordance with Chicago custom, it was to be Daley's function to cut a ribbon in a 12:30 P.M. dedication ceremony, reading a brief speech that someone had written out for him, one of his secretaries making certain when he left his office that the speech was in his jacket pocket.

Midway to the dedication, the Mayor suddenly felt a twinge in his chest. When it persisted, he matter-of-factly told a bodyguard to place a call to the office of Dr. Coogan, his personal physician, informing him that the Mayor would be coming in within an hour or so for a checkup. The call was instantly made on the car phone, but the Mayor looked to be himself again when the limousine pulled up at Mann Park.

About 300 persons were on hand to greet him, headed by Alderman Vrdolyak and Park District Superintendent Edward Kelly. When it came time for Daley to speak, he took the speech from an inner pocket and read: "This buildin' is dedicated to the people of this great community. They are making Chicago a better city, because when you have a good neighborhood you have a good city and this is a good neighborhood." Then, on his own, he wished one and all a merry Christmas and turned to leave. As he did so, someone handed him a basketball and pointed to a nearby hoop. Reflexively, Daley took a shot and, surprisingly, the basketball swished right through. Daley grinned. "Not so bad," he said, "for a kid from Bridgeport." The seventy-four-year-old kid from Bridgeport then drove off to see his doctor.

Arriving at the Michigan Avenue building where Dr. Thomas J. Coogan, Jr., had his offices, Daley jumped out of his limousine and strutted inside, with a cheery wave to the black doorman. As if to impress his bodyguards that there was nothing about his condition to worry them, he trotted up a steep flight of stairs, rather than use an elevator. His bodyguards were accustomed to Daley's engaging in this act of bravado; it was characteristic of him to display his physical fitness by racing up sets of stairs.

The Mayor walked briskly into Dr. Coogan's second-floor offices. He smiled at patients in the waiting room who raised their heads in surprise when he entered; he shook hands with a few of them, exuding confidence. None who saw him had reason to suspect that Daley was not well.

The fact was that for a period of about two weeks, Daley had not been feeling well. It was a secret he shared only with his constant companions, the bodyguards, but he periodically had been brought up short by pains in his chest. On short notice, on two or three occasions, Daley had interrupted his schedule to sneak in a visit to Dr. Coogan. The Mayor appeared to his bodyguards during these two weeks to be introverted and apprehensive, as if in fear that something ominous was happening to him.

Having been alerted that the Mayor was coming in for another checkup, Dr. Coogan was waiting to escort him to a small office. The same symptoms? The sharp pain that came and then passed away? Daley admitted to having felt discomfort earlier in the day. As usual, Dr. Coogan said he had better have a look at him.

Dr. Coogan thought that Daley looked fine. He was disturbed, however, to discover that Daley's blood pressure was elevated. He suggested to Daley that he had been working too hard, perhaps, and that he should be thinking of getting away for a while—that it might not be a bad idea to plan on going to Florida on vacation. The Mayor replied that it was raining in Florida and that the weather down there had been lousy.

In the course of examining the Mayor, Coogan detected a slight atrial fibrillation—an abnormal heartbeat. This was not indicative of an imminent heart attack, but it called for a closer look, and Coogan had Daley stretch out and undergo an electrocardiogram. As Coogan had suspected, the cardiograph confirmed the abnormal heart action. While Daley buttoned up his shirt, fixed his tie, and pulled on his jacket, Coogan talked.

The doctor said that, as a precaution, he thought Daley should get into a hospital for a few days. Daley was not pleased, but he finally said that, if this was what Coogan thought was best, he would do it. When Coogan was leaving the room to make the arrangements for Daley's hospitalization, the Mayor asked if he could make a telephone call to his son Michael, who could convey the news to Mrs. Daley.

It was a few minutes after 2 P.M. when Coogan left Daley to alert the hospital that the Mayor would be checking in shortly. Coogan was astounded to discover, walking back into the examining room two minutes later, that the Mayor was sprawled face down and unconscious on the floor, apparently the victim of a massive heart attack.

Crying out for his associate, Dr. Robert Reid, Coogan rushed to the Mayor's side. They got Daley onto his back and took turns trying to keep him alive with mouth-to-mouth resuscitation. In an outer office, the receptionist, Irene Fahey, was on a telephone line to Fire Alarm.

"We have Mayor Daley in our office, who is having a heart attack!" she cried, a tone of dear-God-please-help-us in her voice.

A Fire Alarm office operator named Sullivan had taken the call on Chicago's "911" emergency telephone line. "Please stay on the line," Sullivan commanded, cutting out for an instant to dispatch the closest available Fire Department ambulance to Coogan's office. The Fire Alarm tape noted that it was at precisely 1416:38 hours on this clear, bone-chilling Monday that the call had been received.

The "911" line is shared by the fire and police communications centers, the operators at police headquarters maintaining silence on fire and ambulance calls, while gauging what police support the emergency might require. Not certain that police communications understood the nature of this call, Sullivan directed his counterpart there, "Please stay on the line. Police dispatcher! Please stay on this line!"

Immediately, a police dispatcher responded: "We have men on the way."

Sullivan then dispatched a second ambulance to 900 North Michigan and then a third. The first, nearest to the point of emergency, had been a basic life-support unit, equipped principally with an emergency inhalator. The other two were sophisticated paramedic ambulances manned by skillful technicians. Sullivan sent two paramedic teams in fear that one might get snagged in traffic.

Assignment editors in the city rooms of the Chicago newspapers and in the newsrooms of the major television stations were brought up short by a sudden jam of activity on their electronic scanners. The scanners are employed to keep continuous watch on the Police and Fire departments' frequencies, the scanning light locking in on any emergency channel that is transmitting. Newsroom people can eavesdrop on the transmissions, simply by turning up the audio, when the little light that patrols these frequencies locks in on any emergency circuit that police and fire communications centers are using to contact personnel in the field.

Scanners have proved to be an invaluable aid to assignment editors, providing them with the most reliable information available on emergencies that require immediate coverage—although, hearing only snatches of police and fire messages that are flying back and forth, editors are sometimes at a loss to determine what it is that they are hearing.

On this December day, the newsroom people were quite perplexed by the extraordinary number of emergency frequencies that sprang to life, the scanning light locking in on each one of them, on the afternoon that Mayor Daley had his heart attack. Something awesome obviously was occurring, but there was no mention of Daley. What in hell, the editors wondered, was going on at 900 North Michigan Avenue?

Nine Hundred North Michigan is in the heart of Chicago's emerging hotel and merchandising center. It is here that Water Tower Place, with its big department stores, innumerable shops, and the top-dollar Ritz-Carlton Hotel, is located, taking the play from famous State Street. The Continental Plaza, the Drake Hotel, the John Hancock Center—there are countless buildings and establishments that have contributed to making North Michigan Avenue the most thriving area in all of Chicago. In Christmas week, 1976, there were mobs of people in the shops and on the Avenue, and something untoward could easily have created panic in such a crowd. North Michigan Avenue was a favorite haunt of business chiefs and other famous people and something might have happened to one of them, provoking the police and fire communications centers to flood the area with emergency vehicles. Something big was happening in the vicinity of 900 North Michigan, this was apparent, but as the minutes dragged on, not an editor or reporter in the city had a clue as to what it might be.

Glaring at a scanner that teased her with indications of a major story in the making, straining to make sense of the garbled messages that she was hearing on police and fire communications, a woman assignment editor in the NBC newsroom in the Merchandise Mart shook her head in pique and said, "God's sakes, why doesn't somebody tell us what it is!" Calls were being placed to phone numbers plucked at random out of the phone book of business firms at 900 North Michigan, no one answering who seemed to know anything—except that a great many squad cars and ambulances were arriving. Then, at about 2:30, capping fifteen minutes of frustration at not knowing what the big story was, the NBC assignment woman got a phone call from a man she knew, who claimed that Mayor Daley had just had a heart attack in Dr. Coogan's office on the second floor of 900 North Michigan.

"Oh, bullshit!" the woman responded. "A crew just came in with film of Daley playing basketball in Vrdolyak's ward, on the South Side." "No bullshit!" the caller insisted; he had been in Coogan's office when Daley had come in—somebody had even said that Daley had run up the stairs rather than use the elevator—and it was true that Daley was there and that he had had a heart attack. None of the other patients got a look at Daley, the man said; but none of them was allowed to leave the office after Daley had the heart attack. Paramedics were working on him at this very moment, the man said. "Jee-sus!" the woman editor exploded, and screamed for reporters and camera crews.

Telephone lines in Chicago were soon alive with calls, as people in all walks of life sought to track down the report that something had happened to the Mayor. Enterprising reporters dialed the phone of Dr. Eric Oldberg, aristocratic president of the Chicago Board of Health. If anybody knew if something had happened to Daley, it would be Oldberg. Hadn't he been the only one, outside the family, who had kept vigil in Daley's room at Rush-Presbyterian-St. Luke's hospital, when Daley had had his stroke in 1974? Dr. Oldberg's secretary said she was sorry, but the doctor could not be reached; he was en route to his home in Lake Forest (a posh North Shore suburb of Chicago).

The area around North Michigan Avenue was vibrating with the cry of sirens, as the first ambulance pulled up to the south entrance of the 900 Building. Shouting a radio message to Fire Alarm: "We are at the scene," the two young medical technicians jumped out to unload their gear. One of Daley's bodyguards, who had been waiting for them, needlessly urged the technicians to be quick. He led them into the building, and the technicians did not delay in reaching the second floor.

Qualified only in basic life-support techniques, the two young men were trained to begin cardiopulmonary resuscitation on a cardiac victim as instantly as they could get to work on him. They found Mayor Daley on his back in an inner office of Dr. Coogan's suite, and judged him to be a victim of cardiac arrest. Trained and authorized to employ electrical shock to a victim's chest, if they found him in a state of ventricular fibrillation—his heart having lost its pulsating rhythm—they swiftly made a try at shocking the quivering muscles of Daley's heart into normal working order.

The medical technicians of the first ambulance were making a heroic effort to revive Daley, when the more highly skilled paramedics—Larry Matkaitis, Dave Gardner, and a trainee named Tom Murphy—arrived with their esoteric equipment and exotic drugs. From experience, the paramedics knew at a glance that Mayor Daley's life was hanging by a thread. Daley still lay flat on his back; his eyes were closed, his mouth was open, and he was motionless. The paramedics instantly took charge. Whatever chance Daley had to live was now in the hands of Matkaitis and Gardner.

It had been on Daley's decision that a great sum of money had been spent on the creation in Chicago of the most elaborate paramedic service in the nation. The concept of young men entrusted with the job of ministering to victims in desperate need, employing electronic wizardry by way of getting immediate instruction from medical doctors in far-off places, was quite beyond Daley's comprehension. The Mayor had only a vague understanding of how the vital signs of stricken persons could instantly be transmitted by the paramedics to doctors who sat in front of electronic screens in the emergency rooms of certain hospitals. It was space-world mumbo jumbo to Daley. Yet, it had been Daley who had decided that however great the cost of such a service might be, it would be well worth the money.

"If it can save lives, the paramedic," Daley had said, "I'm all for it. Why shouldn't we be first, Chicago, when nobody else is doing it? The fellow is having the doctor and there is no doctor, except at the hospitals, these paramedics will do a great job." Thinking perhaps of the old saw that no man knows the day or the hour, Daley had soliloquized, "What's wrong with it, giving the people of this great city something that can save a life? It could be anybody, the one needing help."

Now, on a December afternoon in 1976, inert on the floor of a doctor's office, it was the Mayor himself who was needing help.

Daley was still in his suit jacket when paramedic Matkaitis knelt down to go to work on him. Daley's shirt was unbuttoned, which suggested that the life-support technicians had made an effort to massage the area over his heart as they performed CPR. Whipping a pair of scissors out of a back pocket, Matkaitis swiftly cut Daley's undershirt from bottom to top, baring his chest—ripping it up in order that they could get defibrillator paddles on him quickly, by way of trying to shock his heart into some degree of mechanical activity. Daley was motionless.

As the paramedics knew, Mayor Daley was in an extremely grave condition. His heart muscles were twitching, but his heart had not a semblance of normal function. The situation was desperate, but in these first moments, Matkaitis and Gardner did not despair of saving Daley's life. Many times, through the use of electrical shock and the powerful stimulants that they were trained to employ, they had been successful in such seemingly hopeless cases as this, and they knew that in a high percentage of these cases, death can be averted by the prompt use of electrical shock and strong medication.

Working swiftly, Matkaitis used his scissors to zip through the left sleeve of Daley's $700 House of Duro jacket, ripping it away. Then, opening an intravenous kit from one of the packs that he and Gardner had carried in with them, Matkaitis expertly felt for a strong vein on Daley's bare arm and, finding one, instantly inserled a needle. The Mayor or not, the paramedics were going by the book, and the book said to establish an IV as swiftly as possible, to create a route for medication.

In a cardiac arrest case, the book calls for administering one ampule of sodium bicarbonate, to counteract acidosis. As the contents of a bag of fluid flowed into Daley's arm, via the IV, Gardner and Matkaitis were busy attaching conventional electrocardiogram leads to Daley's chest. Finding him in ventricular fibrillation again, they shocked him once more with the electrical paddles, provoking the heart into a superficial response again. As the electrocardiograph showed Daley slipping back into "fib," Gardner moved to establish communications with the emergency room of Northwestern Memorial Hospital, the nearest hospital participating in the paramedic program. Daley, they knew, was in urgent need of strong medication, and they had to have authorization to administer it—whether on the prostrate Mayor of Chicago, or anyone else.

Only ten minutes had elapsed since Irene Fahey had placed her call to Fire Alarm.

Doctors at Northwestern Memorial were now gathered in front of the telemetry console in emergency, eyes fixed upon the electronic screen that was transmitting electrical printouts from the leads that had been attached to Daley's chest. They could see for themselves that the situation was desperate. In telephone contact with paramedic Gardner, they prescribed the use of the most powerful stimulants in their drug box. Gardner and Matkaitis instantly did what was directed. The Mayor did not respond.

If the battle to save Daley's life was lost, those fighting it were not prepared to surrender. As every effort to provoke a response from Daley's heart failed, they tried something else. Turning to Dr. Coogan, paramedic Gardner said, "I think we need an anestheseologist." Coogan concurred, and in a matter of minutes, a Dr. Barry Shapiro, having been sped over by squad car, arrived in the office where Daley lay.

Working with all possible swiftness, Shapiro slipped a rubber tube into Daley's mouth and worked it down his windpipe—this to provide better ventilation. Whatever thoughts Shapiro had about the futility of this, he got no response from Daley's body; it was as if he had placed a tubing down the throat of a huge, blue-faced doll. He then took a scalpel and, to relieve a pneumothorax—an accumulation of air in Daley's pleural cavity, which was deflating the lungs—made an incision in Daley's chest. There being no sign that this accomplished the slightest good, Dr. Shapiro quietly voiced an opinion to his colleagues that the situation was hopeless.

In the medical profession's pecking order, Shapiro was now the medically responsible doctor in the case, and his opinion that Daley was beyond human help seemed to be the end of the frantic business of trying to save him. Not so.

Shapiro had arrived at Dr. Coogan's at 2:45. Five minutes later, yet another doctor, John H. Sanders, Jr., a thoracic surgeon, walked in, he also having been sped over from Northwestern Memorial by police squad car. By way of keeping Daley's pleural cavity open, Dr. Sanders inserted two tubes into the incision that Dr. Shapiro had made. This availed nothing.

Doctors at Northwestern Memorial instructed the paramedics to resume use of the electrical paddles on Daley's chest. They did, with no visible results. The use of various drugs was ordered—Pronestyl, lidocaine, dopamine. It was useless. Nothing worked.

There were six physicians and surgeons, Daley's son-in-law, Dr. Robert Vanecko, having arrived with the doctor in charge of the Chicago Health Department's medical service, and five Fire Department technicians, including the two paramedics, in the small room where Mayor Daley was laid out on the floor, and nothing that any of them could think of doing had provoked a sign of life.

Talent aplenty and miracles none.

"They gave Dick every chance, hopeless as they knew it was," Dr. Oldberg said later, after reviewing all the data. "He was dead and they all knew it. He was dead when he fell out of the chair and toppled onto his face. They knew it. But, they had to do every damned thing that there was to be done. After all, he was the Mayor."

To cover the contingency that he might be ordered to inject even more medication into the dead Mayor, paramedic Gardner slipped out of the office and downstairs to check out the drugs still available in the ambulance, which had remained parked at the south entrance of the 900 North Michigan Building. The crowd around this entrance had steadily been increasing; as news spread that Daley was dying or dead, attracted by camera crews and other media people who had taken up station near the entrance, people had gathered to witness Daley being carried out.

As paramedic Gardner got to his ambulance, one of the Mayor's bodyguards approached him and ordered him to move the vehicle to the loading dock in the alley on the opposite side of the building, someone in authority obviously having decided that the removal of Daley should not be turned into a spectacle. The crowd, led by the news people, followed the ambulance as Gardner drove it slowly to the loading dock, only to discover that barricades had been placed to keep the public and press at a distance from the place where Daley would be removed from the building. Having backed the ambulance to the loading dock, Gardner went back to Dr. Coogan's office.

There would be work for the paramedics to do, because the room had become increasingly in disarray, as numerous medications were torn loose from their sterile wrappings, used, and then tossed aside. Catheters protruded from Daley's half-open mouth and from the incision that had been made in his chest.

The Daley family had been gathered all this while in a room close to the small office in which the battle to save the Mayor's life was being waged. There had not been a thing that Mrs. Daley and the children could do, save to get on their knees and recite the holy rosary—fearing the worst and submissive to the apparent desire of the doctors that they not be witnesses to the battle.

On his trip back to the office where Daley lay, paramedic Gardner had walked past the room in which Mrs. Daley and the children were waiting. The door was ajar and he observed that members of the family were seated in a composed state. In recounting this later, Gardner said that Mrs. Daley was somber but dry-eyed. "I don't think, at that time, that she had been told her husband was dead."

It was shortly after Gardner had returned to the office, at about 3:40 P.M.—one hour and twenty-five minutes after Irene Fahey had placed her call to Fire Alarm—that the doctors finally conceded that nothing more could be done and that the man who had been hailed as the greatest mayor Chicago ever had was indeed dead.

"We had exhausted every possibility," paramedic Gardner said, in talking of this later. "But, with six physicians on the scene, the decision that the Mayor was dead was made by Dr. Coogan, Dr. Shapiro, and Dr. Sanders. They conferred and agreed that there was absolutely no electrical activity in the Mayor. He showed all indications of biological death at this time. So the doctors gathered up their instruments and left the room, leaving us, the four paramedics, with the body."

The paramedics then placed the body on a stretcher, covering it, except for the face, with a blanket. They then began to clean up the room. "We tried to make him as presentable as possible, in consideration of the family, and we wanted to make the room presentable," paramedic Matkaitis later explained. They intended to place the stretcher on a table and were about to do so when interrupted by a policeman on guard in the adjoining corridor, who opened the office door to permit Father Timothy Lyne of nearby Holy Name Cathedral to come in and bestow upon the dead Mayor the church's blessing for the sick. The paramedics left the room until the priest completed the ritual. Then, when the priest came out, they went back in to resume the cleanup.

It was during this interval that Dr. Coogan was telling Mrs. Daley and the children that the Mayor was dead. He revealed, later, that they appeared to have expected that this was what the news would be and that they seemed already resigned to their loss. As Dr. Eric Oldberg later observed, after he had talked with Mrs. Daley and the children, "It was God's will, according to them. I didn't labor the details in talking about it to Eleanor, Mrs. Daley; obviously, Dick had died almost instantly. He had had a cardiac arrest and he simply had toppled out of a chair and he was dead, perhaps, before he hit the floor. He was dead when he fell. He was dead right then. The good thing was—and this was what I told Eleanor, Mrs. Daley—he didn't suffer. He never knew what had happened to him."

The paramedics were removing the last of their equipment from the room where Daley had died, when the family filed in. It was in silent sorrow that the family gazed upon the dead Mayor, kneeling then to pray for the repose of his immortal soul. No sobbing was heard by anyone outside the closed door— only the subdued voices of people at prayer.

While helping to load gear into his ambulance, paramedic Matkaitis was told by the Mayor's bodyguards that he and Gardner would be transporting the body to the McKeon Funeral Home in Daley's neighborhood, where scores of times across the years Richard Daley had knelt and prayed for the repose of the soul of a Bridgeporter who lay in an open casket. McKeon's was the place where his mother, Lillian, had been waked in 1946, and his father, Michael, in 1959.

It was not until after the family had left the room where Daley lay, returning to the office where they had kept their vigil during the long ordeal, that the paramedics were ordered to remove the body to their ambulance. They were told, "You'll take him out the back way, for privacy." A building custodian was summoned to show them the route, opening doors to a corridor that led to the freight elevators that served the loading dock on the alley side of the 900 North Michigan Building. The blanket was pulled over Daley's face, the muscles getting rigid now, as they carried him out, a Daley bodyguard at their side every step of the way.

Richard J. Daley had died as privately as any great man could. Now, in death, his family seemed intent upon shielding his blanketed remains from the view of curious public and headstrong press. It did not strike any of those who were scheming to get Daley's body into the ambulance unobserved that it was incongruous for the great Mayor of a great city to be removed by freight elevator to an alley-side loading dock.

After the body had been placed in the ambulance, Mrs. Daley and the children were brought down by freight elevator. The media people got hardly a glimpse of the family as they came down the stone steps of the loading dock and quickly got into the Mayor's limousine and a car that had been placed directly behind it—the car of Dr. Robert Vanecko, Daley's son-in-law. Shortly, the cortege began moving out.

The revolving lights of two squad cars came alive and sirens whimpered as the procession pulled out of the alley and headed east in blocked-off Walton Street to Michigan Avenue, where the squad cars in the lead turned right and headed south. The ambulance was directly behind the lead squad cars, paramedic Matkaitis driving, with one of Daley's bodyguards in the seat alongside him. Paramedic Gardner was in the back, with the body. So, also, were trainee Murphy and State Senator Richard M. Daley, the Mayor's eldest son, who was coatless and wearing an open shirt. The limousine was next and then Dr. Vanecko's car and, finally, an unmarked squad car that was on permanent assignment to stay on the tail of the Daley limousine.

To prevent anyone from getting a glance or, worse, a picture of the shrouded body of the Mayor, policemen had placed sections of cardboard box on the inside of the ambulance windows. The only recognizable person in the limousine, in a back seat on the side that faced the news people who had been kept behind the barricades, was Mrs. Daley, head erect and a handkerchief pressed to her lips. Instantly, she had passed from view, as the procession moved out, sirens starting to growl in their menacing way as the cortege picked up speed.

The melodrama was over. Richard J. Daley was being carried south to a funeral home in Bridgeport. This was the last ride he would ever have in Michigan Avenue.

Looking distraught, Frank Sullivan, the Mayor's press secretary, appeared as the sound of the sirens faded. Now, at last, the press was to be told what the condition of Mayor Daley was. Standing bareheaded in the alley, between Don the Beachcomber's restaurant on the one side and a piano bar called The Embers on the other, more than twenty reporters and cameramen crowding him, microphones of newsreel cameras and tape recorders thrust at him by newsmen who pushed and shoved to get within earshot, press secretary Sullivan said, "I am sorry to inform you and the people of Chicago that Mayor Richard J. Daley is dead."

The six-vehicle cortege was already well on the way to Bridge-port, beginning with its five-and-a-half-mile journey in Michigan Avenue. From 900 north to 3500 south, all southbound lanes of the most prestigious thoroughfare in Chicago had been totally cleared of traffic, cops at every intersection. Many motorists, held up at Michigan as they tried to drive across on intersecting streets, honked their automobile horns impatiently—not knowing what reason there might be for the holdup in traffic, or not caring even if they knew. Just as normalcy was already being restored to the area near 900 North Michigan, the crowds dispersing as the body of Daley was carried away, normal traffic was being quickly restored in Michigan, block by block, as the Daley procession passed by.

In tight formation, the Daley cortege moved at a steady but unhurried pace down a route of well-known places that for more than two decades had contributed to the Mayor's joy and pride:

• The historic Water Tower, a sandstone symbol of Chicago's determination to survive—having remained in place as terrible flames of the great fire of 1871 attacked it.

• The neo-Gothic Chicago Tribune tower on the left, and the white-marble Wrigley Building on the right, as the cortege approached Michigan Avenue bridge, taking Daley for the last time over the Chicago River and into the heart of Chicago.

• The 333 Building to the left, on the opposite bank of the river, home of the Tavern Club, where Daley so often had created a flutter of excitement when he dropped in for lunch.

• The dowdy Chicago Public Library building at Randolph Street, still standing despite the Mayor's 1972 plan to tear it down, because Sis Daley—in a rare public protest—had pleaded that this was a part of Chicago that must not be demolished. (Announcing his change of mind, Daley had said, smiling, "She is able to speak for herself very well, whatever she has on her mind.")

• At Monroe Street, on the other side of the Avenue, the grounds of the world-famous Art Institute, two sculptured lions on guard at either side of the main entrance.

• At Adams, Orchestra Hall, home of the renowned Chicago Symphony Orchestra, of which Daley, although hardly a devotee of music, was inordinately proud.

• At Van Buren, the forbidding Chicago Club, snobbish preserve of the men who had made it big in business and finance—a place where Daley had once been regarded by the members as a lout who would bring disgrace upon the city, but where in recent years he had been extravagantly praised and fawned upon.

His kind of town, Chicago was. And down the Avenue he went for a final time.

• At Balbo, the politically historic Blackstone Hotel—where deals had been cut for Warren G. Harding and Franklin D. Roosevelt and Dwight D. Eisenhower and Richard M. Nixon.

• At Balbo, the Conrad Hilton—battleground of the lamentable confrontations of policemen and protesters during Democratic National Convention week, 1968, filling Daley with defiance and grief, indelibly marking him in the minds of many Americans as a tyrant.

• Then down into an all-black residential district that had expanded during Daley's lifetime—save for such zealously guarded white enclaves as Bridgeport—into the Far South Side of the city; the cortege moving more swiftly now.

• At 35th Street, the cortege headed west, passing the hulking ball park of the Chicago White Sox, where Daley, so many days and nights, boyishly had cheered his team.

• At Lowe Avenue, a mile to the west of Michigan, policemen in the police station on the corner, and firemen in their quarters directly next door, peered out the windows as the procession made the turn off 35th and slowly went up the block where Daley had been born and where all of his life he had lived.

The grave faces of many neighbors appeared in the front parlor windows of their frame homes, as the cortege moved down the block. The lead squad car slowed almost to a stop in front of Daley's bungalow. Nevermore would Daley be sitting down at the kitchen table to a good meal, before putting on his dinner jacket and setting out to one of his black-tie affairs for visiting royalty. Nevermore would he be dozing off on a free evening, as he relaxed in his easy chair, amid the front parlor furniture with its plastic slipcovers and the clutter of religious objects, dominated by a big plaster statue of the Virgin. Nevermore.

Matkaitis braked the ambulance at McKeon's Funeral Home. He then jumped out to help Gardner and trainee Murphy carry the stretcher past the bodyguards and the saddened family. A small number of Bridgeport people were standing off at a respectful distance to witness this sad ceremony, many of them wondering what would happen to Bridgeport and all of its City Hall jobs, now that Mr. Clout was dead.

As Mrs. Daley and the children got back into the cars to be driven home, the Mayor's body having been carried in through the receiving entrance of McKeon's, the Bridgeporters silently walked away. The most fateful three hours of Daley's twenty-one-year reign were over.

Chapter Two

"With Daley, you had to be 'one of us' or you got nothing. It is a hell of a way to run a city, but that was how he was."

—Eric Oldberg

DALEY'S PRIVATE LIFE was reserved strictly for the family. Practically nobody got into his home. Dinner was a family affair and Eleanor, 'Sis' Daley, cooked the meals, making bread every day of her life. As a medical man, I thought she fed him too much; he had this tendency, you know, to be a big eater and pick up weight. But mealtime was family time in Daley's house.

"He had a primitive Irish kind of devotion for his wife and his kids and whoever the kids had married. If you want to know something about the *real* Dick Daley, what kind of man he was, you'd have to begin, I think, with his life in the house that nobody got into, out there on Lowe Avenue."

In all the years that Daley had served as mayor of Chicago, in all the dealings he had had with the high and the mighty, his solitary trusted friend was Dr. Oldberg. Theirs was an incongruous friendship.

Oldberg, preeminent neurosurgeon, urbane socialite, aesthete, and Daley, distrustful, arrogant, ignorant if not scornful of artistic things—they were a most unlikely pair to share any accord, the one man knowledgeable in the world of the visual arts and classical music, a gourmet with membership in the most exclu-

21

sive clubs, the other man a master mechanic of politics, having a beer as he cheered the home team at White Sox Park.

Sophisticated Oldberg with his uppercrust Lake Forest background and clipped diction, and his direct way of confronting problems. Back-of-the-Yards Daley, self-conscious in his public appearances, working his political tricks in cunning ways. A strange pair.

"One reason he liked me, I suppose," Oldberg decided, "was that I was an element outside the rather primitive group that he felt comfortable with. He would never have had to ask, say, Bob Quinn the fire commissioner or Bill Lee the union fellow, or any of those guys in his circle, what they thought about something; he knew how they felt. It was automatic; it was born and bred in them to think the same way about everything—including prejudice toward the blacks and things like that.

"I think I represented to him a foothold in an entirely different kind of society and life. I had certain knowledge about the Chicago school system and the Board of Health that was valuable to him. You could say that he needed me; when I came into his life, he had no one else who could provide him with a connection to the 'better' element of the community with whom he had to get along. But he had to accept me on my own terms. There was nothing that I wanted him to do for me. I never took a goddamned thing from Daley because I didn't have to. I would get good and mad at him, when I felt like doing that.

"I wasn't the ideal person to be his friend. I wasn't going to go sucking around, like some of the bankers and the business people; my God, I think that's terrible. But from the very beginning—and we developed a close personal relationship— there was a certain fascination that this man had for me, and I must say that he generated a certain amount of affection from me.

"I knew his faults, as well as his strong points. He had a shrewd intuition about political dealings that I didn't quite comprehend, but he had a certain amount of class to go with it. I wasn't partial to his religious fervor; that was part of the primitive side of him. But he could be charmingly sentimental. Whether he was cultured or not had nothing to do with his brain; whatever anybody would say about Daley, he had a hell of a good brain."

It had been after his election as mayor in 1955 that Daley had latched on to the aristocratic Eric Oldberg. The doctor, chief of neurological surgery of the University of Illinois's Chicago hospitals and the equally distinguished Rush-Presbyterian-St. Luke's Hospital, had for two years served on Mayor Martin H. Kennelly's commission that searched out candidates for the Chicago Board of Education. This was a commission that had been formed to upgrade the quality of those chosen by the Mayor to run the billion-dollar-per-year school system, the board members in the days of Mayor Anton J. Cermak and Mayor Edward J. Kelly having been brazen in their cronyism and boodling.

Some members of Kennelly's commission had flat-out quit when Daley, the Democratic organization's man, had defeated Kennelly in the bitter primary of 1955 and had gone on to win election. The fear was that the election of Daley signified the imminent return of Chicago to the old customs of vice and graft and that fingers would once again be dipping into Board of Education funds.

Dr. Oldberg was not one of those who quit; he preferred to stay on for a while to observe the methods of this unrefined new mayor, whose candidacy had provoked foreboding in the stylish circles of business and society. Perhaps—the doctor thought—this man Daley might not turn out to be as bad as the "better" element feared he would prove to be. From the start, Oldberg said, he had had a desire that this Daley from out in Bridgeport might prove to be a decent sort.

Oldberg had explained to the new Mayor that the commission procedure had been to invite school board nominations from any quarter, that the nominees were then investigated and interviewed and that the names of the most satisfactory of the lot had then been submitted to Mayor Kennelly for his consideration. Dr. Oldberg was pleased that Mayor Daley thought this to be an ideal system for the selection of school board members.

Oldberg was one of the holdovers who had agreed to stay on the search commission, if that was Daley's pleasure. Two years later, Daley asked Oldberg to serve as chairman. He remained as chairman for fifteen years, quitting the job when Daley became so arbitrary that he usurped the power vested in the commission.

"It was a thankless job—long hours and no compensation; only a degree of prestige—serving on the Board of Education," Dr. Oldberg recalled, "but from one source or another we used to get the names of seventy, eighty people who were willing to serve. When we culled the list to about the five or six good prospects that we submitted to the Mayor, it was an implied obligation on the part of the Mayor to fill any vacancies from that list. It had worked that way under Kennelly. Things went smoothly under Daley for about ten years.

"Then—this was at the time that there was so much contention over Superintendent Benjamin Willis, over the black racial thing—the commission recommended that school board members who were openly supporting Willis should not be reappointed when their terms expired. Well, the ones that the commission wanted to get rid of were friends of Daley and he wouldn't hear of getting rid of them.

"I told him, 'Goddamn it, Dick, it won't work—maintaining a school board that is polarized.' I pointed out to him that the situation had become so bad, only a handful of people were now willing to allow their names to be submitted for service on the school board, a thankless job.

"I told him there was no purpose in busy people spending their time screening candidates for the Board of Education, if he insisted upon ignoring the candidates that the commission recommended. But he was obdurate; he bluntly told me that nobody was going to tell him who he could appoint, to the school board or anything else. So, as far as continuing to serve on the commission [was concerned], I told him that I was quitting. I did, but it didn't bother him and, strangely enough, it didn't seem to have an effect on the relationship between us."

In his role as public-spirited citizen, and again because Daley insisted upon having his way in all things, Dr. Oldberg got into conflict with Daley in yet another area. Having accepted appointment to be president of the politically infected Chicago Board of Health, Oldberg was at the point of walking out when Daley brought his elderly family doctor, Morgan O'Connell, out of retirement and appointed him to be assistant city health commissioner.

Oldberg protested that O'Connell was devoid of background in dealing with problems of public health and was utterly unqualified, but Daley argued that he was only trying to do a kindness for the man who had delivered all seven of his children—an old Bridgeport friend who needed a little boost in his golden years. Daley assured Oldberg that O'Connell would in no way infringe upon Oldberg's effort to inject professional efficiency into an agency that was disgracefully in need of it. Subsequently, Oldberg was furious when Daley elevated the grossly inadequate O'Connell to the post of commissioner of the Department of Health.

Unwilling to submit meekly to Daley's arrogance, Oldberg contrived a showdown in the mayor's office between Daley and an eminent delegation of medical people and hospital administrators. Daley pushed back in his chair, folded his arms, and smoldered as this professional group served an ultimatum on him that the welfare of the people of Chicago demanded that Dr. O'Connell be sacked. Finally, Daley exploded in defense of his old friend—shouting, irrationally, that those gathered in his office did not represent the people of Chicago, that all they wanted to do was dirty up the reputation of a good man, that they had better remember that *he* had been elected to decide what was best for Chicago—

"I was tempted to quit, right then, as president of the Board of Health," Dr. Oldberg recalled; "this had been mortifying. I didn't quit because I believed that there was urgent need to shape up the city's health program—and I had a fear that if I refused to continue in this task, who would? It made me furious to have to work within these political parameters, but I felt an obligation to stay in the post, 'Commissioner' O'Connell or not, and do whatever I could."

In time, the political and administrative ineptitude of Dr. O'Connell—especially his failure to clear with Daley the hiring and firing of health department personnel—became too much for even Daley to bear and the family doctor was sent back to retirement, this time with a city pension. Dr. Oldberg selected his replacement, a man of some experience in the field of public health. It had been highly unusual, however, for Daley to have allowed Oldberg to have the option in this selection.

"It was always fascinating to observe how Daley zealously guarded his appointive power; in all of his years as mayor, he would allow nobody to take it away from him." His power, Dr. Oldberg perceived, "was largely based upon the fact that every goddamned person that had anything to do with running any department in the city of Chicago was beholden to Dick Daley for the job that he held. Every one of them. He made every appointment down to the fourth echelon; he either made it personally or he approved it. Everybody who got one of the city jobs knew that he got it because Dick had OK'd it.

"If you'd go to him with a name of somebody you thought was qualified to fill an opening, he would never give you an answer right at that moment. He would say, 'Fine, Doc, I think you have given me a fine name,' or something like that. He said he would look into it. And it might be the next day or it might be six months before he appointed your person or somebody else, and in the meantime he wouldn't have said a damned word to you about it. He wanted you to know that giving out jobs was entirely within his hands, that it was Richard J. Daley who ran the whole goddamned show. All of the decisions on hiring went to the fifth floor, to his office—every damned time. You didn't make any appointments without clearing it with him. You would suggest something or somebody to him, but he made the decision. And, in one way or another, all of the decisions were political.

"I had a nurse in charge of nurses at the Board of Health and when she retired, I wanted another one as good as this one. So when the one who was retiring recommended someone else, I checked it over and the new one looked quite acceptable to me and so I brought a dossier on her over to Daley. He said, 'Fine, Doc; I'll look into it.' Well, I heard nothing.

"Weeks went by and I needed this head nurse and I heard nothing. So finally I had someone who was in a position to find out what had happened check up on this thing for me. Basically, I wanted to find whether this woman would be appointed by

Daley or not. Well, we found out that the dossier went from Daley to Donovan—Tom Donovan of Bridgeport, the patronage kid. We found out that Donovan checked where the woman voted—out on the West Side, at the medical center. Donovan discovered that she had voted in the 1975 primary and had asked for a Democratic ballot, when it was Daley against Billy Singer, the liberal anti-Daley alderman and a couple of other guys—Dick Newhouse, the black state senator, and Eddie Hanrahan, the former state's attorney.

"Well, when the election came on April 1st of 1975, when it was Daley against John Hoellen, the Republican, this woman didn't vote. *A priori*—Donovan's logic—she must have voted for Singer, or maybe Newhouse or Hanrahan, in the primary. Donovan's conclusion was that if she had voted for Daley in the primary, she would have done so again in the election with Hoellen. Only, she didn't. Therefore, she was out and Daley wouldn't let her have a job on the Board of Health. That's typical of the way they checked things out; that's the way, under Daley, it worked.

"There was no point in my going to Daley to argue that maybe there was a reason she didn't vote in the election, that maybe she was out of town on election day or something like that. They simply assumed that she voted for Singer, or one of the others, in the primary and she wouldn't vote for Daley in the election with Hoellen and she was out. In Daley's thinking, 'She's not one of us.' With Daley, you had to be 'one of us' or you got nothing. It is a hell of a way to run a city, but that was how he was."

On rare occasions in Daley's nearly twenty-two years as mayor, the business and financial community forced decisions upon him.

In 1960, it had been in fear of losing favor with the monied crowd that Daley reluctantly resolved a humiliating disclosure of corruption in the Chicago Police Department. With political misgivings, he found himself maneuvered into accepting an erudite criminologist that the power bloc had forced upon him— Orlando W. Wilson of the University of California at Berkeley— to restructure the department. Not only did this entail surrender of his despotic control over the police; it led also, as Daley had feared it might, into a quadrupling of the department's $72-million budget to fund the increases of wages, introduction of a sophisticated communications system and other expenditures that Wilson insisted upon.

During the 1960s, Daley had ignored the black community's revulsion toward the school segregation policies of Superintendent Benjamin Willis. But finally Daley had been forced to accede to the subtle pressures of the powerful interests of Chicago that, to avoid an outbreak of grave racial conflict in the city, he would have to negotiate a settlement with the Reverend Dr. Martin Luther King, Jr., and, though his heart wasn't in it, he made a well-publicized effort to pacify Dr. King.

A great deal of the desperation that propelled Daley into wild shoot-to-kill talk, during the West Side riots that erupted in the spring of 1968, following the assassination of King in Memphis, Tennessee, could be placed on his fear that the most important people in Chicago were suspicious that he was losing control of the city.

It had been with dread that Daley contemplated what the judgment of the "better" element might be, when his overreaction to the anti-Viet Nam war demonstrators, during the August 1968 Democratic Convention in Chicago, shocked the nation.

Yet, there were times when Daley had been indifferent to criticism or rebuke.

It had not impressed Daley that Eric Oldberg and the medical societies were in despair over his placing executive control of the Chicago Health Department in the inept hands of Morgan O'Connell, his family physician.

When one of his prominent admirers—Fairfax Cone of Foote, Cone & Belding, a major advertising agency—tore from a Chicago newspaper a picture of the Mayor and First Ward Democratic Committeeman John d'Arco, the crime syndicate's man, sending it to Daley with an angry message, scribbled in advertising agency crayon—"How can I be for you, when you're for people like this?"—there was not a flicker of reaction from Daley.

On a day-by-day or year-by-year scale, it was often impossible to separate the Jekyll from the Hyde in Richard Daley. His attitude seemed to be that he was providing the people of means with the kind of city they wanted—not too much scandal, reasonably good services, a tax base that was not oppressive, an adequate and docile work force, a rather good public transit system—and it was none of their business how he accomplished this.

He had a psychological resistance toward any infringement on the prerogatives that he held to be his alone. It was always with deep resentment, and never with an open admission that someone else had better judgment than his own, that Daley was ever persuaded to do something that he did not want to do.

"We had a bit of a problem with him back in 1972," Eric Oldberg recalled. "It was his intention to go to the Democratic Convention in Miami Beach, to fight for his right to take his place in the proceedings down there. Many of us in Chicago were disturbed about this, even though we were all Republicans. We knew damned well that he would be embarrassed. He was licked already, before he went. His delegation was not going to be seated; it was apparent to even outsiders like ourselves that the sentiments of those in control of that convention were against letting him in.

"There had been a good deal of talk among some of us about this. It didn't much matter to most of those who talked about this in the clubs—the Chicago Club, at the Casino, and so on—as to what damage that Daley would do to himself, but we were all pretty damned concerned over what damage his trip down there might do to our city.

"So, one Saturday a lot of us were out on the big yacht that the Illinois Tool Works owns, a huge big thing; we were having an outing for pals of the company president who were members of the Chicago Club—drinks and a hell of a lunch and so on—and we went out and traveled up and down the shore, and the fellows got together and talked about one thing or another; and when we were back at the dock and the fellows were getting off, Hal Grumhaus of the *Tribune* and Brooks McCormick of International Harvester got hold of me. Hal came right out with it. He said, 'We've been talking it over and we don't think that

Dick Daley ought to try to go to Miami. He just shouldn't do that and we think that you're the man to persuade him not to do it.'

"Well, this was on a Saturday and most of the Illinois people, these Democrats, had left for the Convention, even though they weren't going to get in. Daley's plan was to fly down the next morning, but I said I would see what I could do.

"Democratic headquarters were still located then in the Sherman House and I went to a public phone and arranged to meet Daley over there in his inner office. I told him straight out, 'Dick, a lot of your good friends in Chicago, Republicans, don't want you to go to Miami.' Well, he just sat back and looked at me. So I said, 'Dick, you're going to be humiliated and you'll humiliate Chicago and that's what they're worried about; they don't want Chicago and its mayor to be humiliated by that bunch down there. There'll be a bunch of hippies waiting for you—hollering and yelling and raising hell down there—and your friends here in Chicago just don't think you should be there.'

"Well, he thought this over for a minute and then he said, 'Doc, I know I shouldn't go directly to Miami; I'm going to fly to [Fort] Lauderdale and be driven down to Miami.' I shook my head at him and said, 'That won't make a damned bit of difference; they'll all know it when you get there and it won't do you any good. You'll be holed up in a hotel room with the Democrats who are down there and there will be demonstrations outside, day and night, and the television people will feast on this stuff.' He tried to argue with me that the demonstrators wouldn't pick him out as a target, so I said, 'Listen to me, Dick, your friends here in Chicago—they've got their people down there. Hal Grumhaus has good information on what the situation is, and everybody here in Chicago is agreed that you'll just be humiliated if you go.'

"I talked to him for three hours. He wouldn't budge; he was going, that's all there was to it. But he finally said, 'Well, I'll go home and think about it. I'll call you up tonight about it, whether I am going or not.' That was not the answer I wanted, so when he got up to go across the street, to City Hall, I went along with him, talking all the while.

"Up in his office on the fifth floor, he shut the door and so I suggested that he talk to Grumhaus about it. Well, he said OK, he would do that. This being a Saturday, when people have busy calendars, there was no telling where Grumhaus might be. We had a hell of a time finding him, but finally I managed to get him on the phone, told him where I was, and put him on the phone with Dick. I couldn't hear what Hal was telling him, but Dick didn't argue or anything; he was sort of meek. But, after he finished talking to Grumhaus of the *Tribune,* he still wouldn't say he wouldn't go.

"So I argued with him for another hour and then Daley said, 'Well, Doc, maybe you're right. Maybe I shouldn't go.' So I said, 'Well, now are you going to call me tonight, at home?' And he said, 'No, I don't think I have to do that. You have my word on it, I won't go.'

"So when I got home, I turned on the television and heard them reporting that Mayor Daley of Chicago had sneaked into town, down there in Miami Beach, and was holed up somewhere, plotting to get into the convention. Like hell he was; he was already over in his place in Michigan and that's where he stayed until the convention was over."

Since he had acquired it in the early 1960s, Daley had periodically secluded himself in his spacious second home, as he was doing during Democratic convention week of 1972. Two years later, following his endarterectomy, when all of Chicago had been gripped by the question of whether Daley would live or die—whether, if he survived, he would be functional and capable of remaining as mayor—it was again to his summer estate in Grand Beach, on the shores of Lake Michigan, that Daley had fled. It had been here, in a home as well guarded as that of a chief of state, set in seven acres secure from all intruders, that Daley had remained in isolation for the four summer months of 1974. The doctors who had performed surgery on his left carotid, clearing blockage that was impairing blood flow to his brain, had been concerned over the high level of anxiety in their seventy-two-year-old patient, and were pleased that he took ample time, about three weeks, to relax before the ordeal.

It had not in the least surprised the cardiovascular experts at

Chicago's Rush-Presbyterian-St. Luke's Hospital that the delicate operation, scheduled for a Monday morning, had been moved up a day on orders of the apprehensive Mayor; they knew he was unpredictable. The surgeons did not understand the reason Daley might have had for demanding a change of schedule, and never got an explanation of it. But just as Daley had not confided in them, the surgeons decided among themselves, Dr. Eric Oldberg concurring, that nothing was to be gained by informing Daley that his right carotid had been discovered to be totally blocked and quite beyond surgical repair. Indeed, Daley went to his grave not knowing that for an extended period of time, he had been functioning on the blood supply of one carotid, not two.

The public was never informed and the press was left to speculate, but the operation had left Daley in a weakened condition and with temporary impairment of his muscles and his speech, and it took him an extended period to make a recovery. It would have been devastating to his ego for anyone outside his family to know that he had been damaged.

Following the operation, it had troubled Daley that he had to search his mind for words and that he had difficulty expressing the words. It worried him that he could not sign his name with the old flourish, and he worked on that. In Daley's world, he had to mix with people and give speeches, and he was determined that he would not return to public view until he was "all right," meaning until he was fully recovered. Learning through their grapevine that Daley, who had always been satisfied to express himself in fractured sentences, was striving to regain his ability to speak, top Democrats joked that a terrible thing had happened to Daley: now that he had had the operation, people might be able to understand what he was saying.

By no means did Daley abandon control of City Hall during his long convalescence. There was a continual flow of information, reports and documents, between the Mayor and his department heads. With Tom Donovan keeping him advised of every important problem that arose in City Hall, Daley managed to maintain pressure on all who worked for him. The requirement was that if you worked for Daley, you did what you were told to do and you did it quickly. Those who had been placed in key positions by Daley were in grim agreement that he was demanding, impatient, and sometimes ruthless.

The tension of working for Daley could be enormous. On one occasion, Deputy Mayor Kenneth Sain had gone to Dr. Oldberg, complaining of frightful headaches that he feared were the product of a brain tumor. Even after Oldberg examined him and assured him it was anxiety, fed by fear that, working for Daley, he might be caught in a bad mistake, Deputy Mayor Sain insisted upon having a sophisticated and expensive brain scan that he had to pay for.

Richard J. Daley lived by his own rules. You said absolutely nothing to anybody, when it was possible to say nothing. You kept a distance from everyone. When someone started getting close to you, you made a point of shutting him off. It was a trick of survival for Daley to display personal interest, say, in one of the young aldermen, making it appear that he was suddenly the Mayor's favorite—and then, just as suddenly, switch him off and turn the favor of his attention upon someone else. As Eric Oldberg said, "It was fantastic to watch the way he could do that, playing one man against another man. It was like watching a good chess game, to see him cater to one guy and then drop him and cater to his rival. This was his technique in not letting anybody get too close to him. What it amounted to was that he simply didn't trust anybody."

One of Oldberg's painful experiences with Richard Daley concerns an occasion when it appeared that Daley was attempting to terminate their association. "For some reason or other, he began to ignore me. He suddenly became too busy to take my phone calls and he couldn't seem to fit me into his schedule when I had something important that I wanted to talk to him about. I couldn't understand it, because I hadn't asked to be a close adviser to him—that was what *he* had wanted. How do you react when a man who has asked for your advice on every damned thing—a man who has insisted that you come to his house for a cup of tea, when he didn't invite anybody else to his house—a man who has talked to you about his health and his kids—how do you react when he cuts you off for no reason?

"When my son, George, died, one of the Mayor's cars pulls into the driveway of my house in Lake Forest and this body-guard pops out with two loaves of bread and a baked ham that Eleanor Daley had just fixed— How do you explain the action of a guy who had wanted to be this close to you, cutting you off with no reason? Well, I'll tell you, it made me goddamn mad and I told him so.

"I wrote him a letter and I told him, 'You're neglecting me and I don't like it. If you think you've pensioned me off or something, so be it, but I want you to know that I don't like it.' I sent that letter out to his house by messenger and I was curious as to how he might respond. Well, he called me up when he read the letter and he asked me to come over right away and when I walked in on him, he had this contrite look on his face and he said, 'Oh, that letter! I was shocked. What made you think I'm not grateful for all you have done for me?' Hearing this from a man who had been acting as if he wanted to break off association with me, *I* was shocked. Some of my friends occasionally asked me what Dick Daley was really like. How do you explain what kind of man he was? How do you 'explain' a guy who vacillates like that?"

Daley had chortled when the Soviet news agency, Tass, once took a stab at answering the question "On what is Daley's power based?" Tass provided accurately a part of the answer when it said, "In the first place, Daley has the complete confidence of Chicago's bankers, industrialists, landlords, and the local press. Secondly, he has at his disposal the municipal machine, with as many as 100,000 jobs, and he is sure to provide his adherents with lucrative jobs." But principally, Tass said—taking note that Daley had won reelection to a fourth four-year term in 1967 with 74.4 percent of the vote, to a fifth four-year term in 1971 with 70.1 percent of the vote—"in Chicago, the crooked manipulation of the ballot decides the elections. If the final tallies do not come out for 'the city's father,' they can always be altered."

Tass was on target, of course, in crediting Daley's survival in large measure to the accommodation he had with the moneyed people. Tass was wildly exaggerative in fixing the patronage he controlled at 100,000 jobs; the hard-core figure was only about one third of that. Tass was patently misinformed in the charge that crooked elections had anything to do with his automatic reelections. Undeniably, ward bosses who curried his favor contrived in every fashion to fatten up the vote that Daley got over his nondescript opponents. But the enigmatic Soviets were too simplistic in their solution to the riddle of why, time after time, overwhelming numbers of Chicago voters preferred Daley over anyone who presumed to run against him.

There was logical reason for the people of Chicago to have had misgivings about retaining Richard Daley as mayor, when he consented to stand for reelection once again in 1975. Supposedly, he was bowing to the desires of the business community and the Democratic organization politicians that he make the great sacrifice of seeking a sixth term. The balance sheet did not support the presumption, however, that he was the indispensable man.

Not only was he still recovering from arterial surgery that had almost done him in, a short half-year earlier, but he was on the far side of his seventy-second birthday and he was confronted by many problems when in December of 1974 he favored his adoration society with the announcement that he would run again. He was beset by racial troubles in an all-white area of the city known as Marquette Park; he was under continual attack as a racist by black Congressman Ralph Metcalfe; and his police department had been accused in federal court of maintaining illegal surveillance on respectable citizens who were critical of his administration. His city was being denied access to $94 million of federal revenue-sharing funds by a judge who decreed that Chicago was not entitled to this money until it stopped its willful practice of discrimination in the hiring of policemen and firemen.

Worried about the cash position of his city, Daley had rammed through the City Council approval of a $55-million loan of dubious legality, there being no precedent for borrowing of this kind. Daley had been abjectly grateful to his obsequious new pal A. Robert Abboud, chairman of the mighty First National Bank, for working out the deal whereby it would be possible for the "city that worked" to pay the bills it had been budgeted to pay out of the federal revenue-sharing funds that it could not now touch; yet, barring a change of heart on the part of a judge who seemingly was immovable on the discrimination issue, Daley was weighted with worry as to where he could scratch up the money to pay off the debt.

Confronted by a strike of 22,000 public school teachers who were demanding more pay, Daley ignored his pretense that he would never interfere in Board of Education business and dictated the granting of a wage increase of $58 million, even though he was quite aware that the school board had no foreseeable sources of revenue to meet it.

Politically, the United States attorney, James R. Thompson, who had put so many members of Daley's machine in prison on graft and corruption charges, was confidently gearing up to run as the Republican candidate for governor on an anti-Daley platform. The smirking anti-Daley incumbent, Dan Walker—the man who sprang to fame as head of a presidential commission on violence that had slashed Daley with its conclusion that his administration had incited a police riot during the lamentable 1968 Democratic Convention in Chicago—was already goading Daley to stop him from winning reelection in 1976, if Daley could contrive to stop him.

There was hardly a possibility that the voters of Chicago would deny Daley a mandate in 1975 to carry on for another four years. He was, beyond question, the most powerful politician the city had known; his machine had a solid grip on the city-wide vote; the labor bosses were intensely loyal to him; the commerce and industry crowd shamelessly kissed his bottom.

There was a chance, of course, that he might suddenly be stricken or die. As Dr. Oldberg observed, "If the left carotid blocks off and it isn't taken care of right away, it will be like cutting his head off; he'd be decerebrate. He doesn't give any thought to the possibility that this might happen; he seems to think that he is recovered from the first experience and that his body is working OK, and it is, and it doesn't seem to enter his mind that, poof! he could go like that." Dr. Thomas Coogan, Daley's physician, had prescribed a diuretic for Daley, Hydrodiuril, to induce the passing of water to lower the blood volume and keep his blood pressure from soaring, which it was inclined to do when, not infrequently, he got angry. Otherwise, apart from his postoperative habit of sneaking home every afternoon for a two-hour nap, Daley was following the same regimen of moderate living that he had followed before he was stricken.

At his age, approaching seventy-three, and having been in the public eye so long, another man might have welcomed a chance gracefully to step aside. Daley's total absorption, however, was in holding the office of mayor. It was an exalted office, apart from the perquisites of Cadillac limousines, bodyguards, rubbing shoulders with the mightiest men in the land, hosting formal dinners for visiting royalty, handing out plaques of honorary citizenship to the astronauts, the Bob Hopes, the Henry Kissingers, and all the others who came to his office for an audience. Daley was captivated by the prestige that was his by virtue of being the mayor and quick to take offense at even innocuous remarks that he regarded as disrespectful to the office he so vainly held.

In public, Mrs. Daley and the children invariably referred to him as The Mayor, in much the same way that the family of a monarch would refer to the head of the household as the king. It was an enormous accomplishment, in Daley's mind, to be mayor of Chicago; it was as great an achievement to hold office as mayor of Chicago as any achievement a man could have. And he guarded the dignity of this office like a jealous lover.

Indeed, he had made his sensitivity clear in the first days following his election in 1955. It was largely with the funding and support of organized labor that his election over Mayor Martin H. Kennelly had been made possible, and his longtime pal William Lee of the Teamsters union had rendered invaluable help in bringing off this coup. Yet, when the newly elected Mayor walked into his first civic luncheon tardy, after everyone else had been seated, Daley glared at his friend when Bill Lee gently chided him, "You're late, Richard." The benediction of this luncheon had scarcely been given, when Daley confronted the union leader and warned him, "Don't you ever call me 'Richard' in public. *I am the Mayor,* and don't you ever forget it."

Daley, of course, was more than just the mayor of Chicago.

He was concurrently the Democratic Party boss of the city, and this is quite another area of authority. It troubled a great many people in Chicago that he so greedily clutched both jobs. Democratic politicians grumbled that Daley had taken control of all the spoils. And there was disquietude in the top-drawer clubs. It was all very well to lend support to an unpolished sort of man who seemed to be doing an acceptable job of running the city, but rather distasteful for the fellow to be flopping around simultaneously as the biggest fish in the partisan pool of Democratic politics.

The approval, if not pride, that the upper crust had come to have in Mayor Daley was somehow qualified by the man's ward-boss yammering. However acceptable a mayor Daley might have proved to be, the moneyed people of Chicago were not comfortable with the political-boss side of him. They had looked with dread upon Daley's rise to power. The business and financial interests had been pro-Martin H. Kennelly, and they viewed Daley's part in the machine's scuttling of the businessman-mayor as an invidious scheme to drag sweet Chicago down to the gutters of vice and corruption where its reputation had wallowed in the Kelly-Nash era—Pat Nash having been the city's Democratic boss when Daley was a mere precinct captain. There was, in short, a disturbing side to the image of Richard J. Daley as the greatest of all mayors.

A quiet kind of anguish had engulfed the "better" element of Chicago, the business people and the social-register set, when the boorish Democrats had turned on Martin Kennelly. It was to Kennelly that they had appealed in 1947, when it became clear that someone of respectability would have to be elected in Mayor Edward J. Kelly's place, if the Democrats were to retain control of the city. For two terms, eight years, the soft-spoken, quasi-cultivated Kennelly had labored to cleanse Chicago's reputation. For what other reason, other than a desire to slip back into the arms of whoring, graft, and gambling, would the organization Democrats—under a new chairman, Daley—plot to knife the gentle Kennelly?

It was unthinkable that the mayoral candidacy of Daley, who looked to be nothing more than a Back-of-the-Yards boor, could be anything other than a portent of evil days to come. Gravely worried about the future of Chicago, Eric Oldberg and many others gave substantial campaign contributions to Kennelly, and those who could, went to the polls on primary day to vote for him. A pall settled over the upper-income people of Chicago when Daley, with his blustery speeches about Chicago's need for dynamic leadership, defeated Kennelly by a substantial margin. With Daley now facing an election with a bright young man named Robert Merriam on the Republican side, Oldberg's crowd got behind Merriam. Again, they lost. It appeared that Chicago was in for a bad time.

As a leading citizen who had worked hard to screen for Kennelly top-grade candidates for the Board of Education, this having been a choice preserve for graft during Ed Kelly's thirteen years as mayor, Oldberg had occasion early in Mayor Daley's term to call on him and ask what his pleasure might be in the matter of school board elections. Oldberg walked into Daley's office with misgivings. One of the few people from his crowd who had an opportunity to take a closeup look at the new mayor, Oldberg had entered Daley's office in an analytical frame of mind.

He had been immediately taken aback by Daley's softspoken courtesy, by his expression of thanks to Oldberg for the efforts the doctor had made in searching out good people for the school board, by Daley's unqualified desire that Oldberg remain on the screening committee. When Oldberg, testing Daley, ventured a compliment to the nonpolitical style of Martin Kennelly, Daley responded that it would be a rule with him not to conduct political business in the mayor's office. Somewhat relieved, Oldberg took his leave.

In short order, he was passing on word to his friends that the new man did not have the personal charm of Kennelly, but he did not appear to be too bad a sort. Oldberg's judgment was that this Daley "might in fact prove to be quite a decent kind of fellow—fair, honest, and so on." And thus began a friendship that deepened with the passing of the years.

"I was never blind, of course, to the contradictions and the inconsistencies that I found in Daley," said Dr. Oldberg. "I think he had too high a toleration point for what some of the people around him were doing. He knew what was going on, of course; he was no damn fool. He knew what Tom Keane was up to and others. He was a realist. But unless something that was far out of line came directly to his attention, well, he would pretend he didn't know about it. If something came directly to his attention and he feared that he was going to be hurt, wham! out the fellow would go.

"He could be ruthless, if he had to be. But, mostly, he took these kinds of things in stride and wasted no emotion on them. He showed no emotion about Tom Keane getting caught and sent to prison, for example. I had the idea that he felt that guys like Keane had let him down and committed crimes that made him look bad, so he didn't have to shed any tears over them. Sometimes, I thought he had too much patience with some of these people.

"Take Matt Danaher. What was it that a federal grand jury indicted Danaher for—a quarter-of-a-million-dollar real estate deal, or something on that order? Well, Daley tolerated Matt Danaher long after he should have. He had been with Daley, of course, from the earliest days; he was the patronage chief for Daley; Daley made him an alderman and county clerk [sic] and all the rest of it; they were neighbors—my God, Matt lived right down the block from Daley. But he began to drink and left home and it got to be pretty awful. Even so, the Mayor stuck with him.

"Then they find him in his shorts, sprawled out on the floor of his hotel, the way it happens with men who drink a lot—always falling down and busting their heads. Then, at the end, there was the Mayor as a pallbearer at Matt's funeral. I didn't go; I saw the film of it on TV, Daley helping to shove the casket into the hearse and all of that. I thought, watching this, that Daley was saying to himself, 'Well, the poor devil, I'm sorry for what happened to him.' But Daley was the kind of man who could mix sentiment with ruthlessness; he had a strange way of combining these two things. You would see him cut someone off in his tracks and then, later, tears would come quickly to him when he spoke about the fellow. So I had this feeling, watching television, that Daley was really glad to be shoving Danaher's casket into the hearse and being finished with him. It was his way to be glad in a situation of this kind."

Just as Daley had had a paternal affection for Matt Danaher, until disillusioned by Matt's behavior, Daley frequently indulged in a similar sort of blind loyalty in other areas. A major league baseball fan from the time he was a little boy and sat in the bleachers with his father, Mike, Daley had neighborhood pride in the Chicago White Sox, whose park was not far from the block in Bridgeport where Daley had been born and where all of his life he had lived, but only a touch of civic pride in the Chicago Cubs, who played in Wrigley Field, on the North Side of the city. Gazing at a game from his box in Wrigley Field, Daley would point and critique the manner in which this player was swinging a bat, or some other player was guarding the third-base line, the tone of Daley's voice suggesting that somebody should tell the lad what he was doing wrong. In White Sox Park, no hometown player was ever discovered by Daley to be doing anything wrong; instead, he would offer an anecdote, complimentary, about various players—sometimes pointing toward a player as he said, "See that fella? He's a great family man"—which was, of course, as nice a thing in Daley's scale of values as you could say about a man.

If, as some said, an enthrallment with his ancestry was part of the primitive side of Daley, some of his acquaintances in the business community felt uncomfortable when "invited" by Daley to buy tickets to banquets at which Daley raised money for the poor souls in Ireland. It was part of the drill that Daley was likely to ask anyone to do anything and that you had better do what he wanted, if you cared to stay on his good side; but it was likewise true that Prime Minister Liam Cosgrave of Ireland, attending one of these Daley-sponsored dinners, had remonstrated with the Mayor that much of his well-intentioned charity was winding up in the bombs-and-guns fund of the IRA (Irish Republican Army). Not dissuaded, Daley raised quite a good deal of money for the Irish; Colonel Jack Reilly, who ran these affairs and arranged for the transfer of these funds to Ireland, admitted to a net profit of $300,000, so it had to be at least that much. Even so, it is further evidence that when Daley was rooting for the home team, he made no secret of where his heart was.

"Part of the frustration of trying to be helpful to Daley," Dr. Oldberg said, in reflecting on the dead Mayor's career, "was this predilection he had to preserve his own privacy. It is impossible to diagnose what is troubling a man, or suggest a cure, when he is so guarded that he won't tell you the truth of what is bothering him. He didn't want anybody around him who would be questioning his judgment. I think this is why he kept a distance from Tom Keane. I think this is why he kept narrowing the circle of people who got close to him to primitives like himself who would be afraid to contravene his judgments.

"I wondered sometimes why he wasn't more particular about the class of people with whom he surrounded himself. I couldn't figure out how Daley got mixed up with these kinds of people. A lot of these funny relationships, grubby real estate developers and crooked road builders and such as that, were brought on by his desire to fix things up for his kids; these were people who were being nice to the Daley kids and, of course, Dick was promoting the kids all of the time. Whatever they might be, if they were helping his kids they were all right in Dick's mind. It was amazing, though, the types that he got mixed up with.

"There was the damnedest bunch around when one of the kids got married—the son who married the Italian girl whose father was tied up in some way with the crime syndicate crowd. Some of them threw a bridal party for the Daleys at the Drake Hotel and I was there, with my wife, and I couldn't figure out how in hell Dick ever got mixed up with such people, because they were the crudest, cheapest-looking group you ever saw in your life. But apparently they had a lot of money and that made them acceptable."

Although there were areas of Daley's private affairs into which Oldberg dared not intrude, he had no reticence in pressing Daley for justification for his exercising autocratic control of Chicago's political machinery. Oldberg's crowd had never become reconciled to Daley's insistence upon holding total political control of Chicago, and Daley had consistently evaded the question. "We were disturbed, myself and my friends," Oldberg said, "that he considered it proper to retain all political power in his own hands. You know, in 1953 he was elected chairman of the Democratic Central Committee, giving him enormous power. Then, in 1955, he was elected mayor, giving him control of everything else. Satisfactory mayor that he proved to be, it struck many of us that this was not a healthy situation for the city, all the political power in control of one man.

"When I became increasingly close to Daley, my friends continually approached me with the question of how he could possibly justify holding all of this power. So I would put the question to him and for a long time—for years—he evaded the question. Finally, one day he studied me and said, 'Doc, when I got to be the mayor, everybody told me I had to give up the other. Everybody told me you couldn't do that, get away with holding both jobs, mayor and chairman. Jack Arvey, who had been runnin' the Democratic party, Joe Gill, who was chairman before I got it; the newspapers—they kept sayin', you can't do that, both jobs. It has never been done, they said; if you're the mayor, you can't be the other. So I thought a lot about this and wondered what I should do.'"

What Daley decided to do, according to Oldberg, was go home and talk it over with his wife. "It was not well known, but Daley used to talk over everything with Eleanor. She was a strong woman. She didn't make Dick's decisions, I'm certain, but he always told her what he was doing or planning to do. She was always quite well aware of things. They discussed everything privately, deciding what was the best course for Dick to take. In this case, Dick said, 'I talked to Sis about it, what people were saying, and then we have this blackboard in the basement and we went down in the basement and I got out the chalk and we list it all on the blackboard as we think of things, the plus side and the minus side of keeping both jobs, or giving one up. When it is all on the blackboard, we discuss it and we finally decide: how can you do a good job as the mayor, unless you've got the other job to slate the candidates who run for the offices and make the appointments? Who says it has to be done the other way, holding only one job? They don't know, [those] who say it, because they never had the chance of doing it.' You can dispute the logic of Daley's argument," his friend Oldberg said, "but that is all the explanation I ever got out of him as to why he insisted on running a one-man show."

An ultimate benefit of running the whole show was that you could slate yourself for high office, or not slate yourself, as you pleased. It had been part of the plan of the Jake Arveys and the Tom Keanes, the powerful Alderman Keane then emerging as a Democrat of consequence, and others of high station in the Democratic hierarchy of Chicago, that the election of Dick Daley to be party chairman in 1953 was to be followed by choosing him to be organization candidate for mayor in 1955, expecting him then to resign as chairman. In a pretense of disqualifying himself from having a voice in choosing the candidate in 1955, chairman Daley excluded himself from the slatemaking committee that he appointed to interview mayoral hopefuls. It was typical of Daley, however, to take a seat in a corner of the private room where potential candidates, including incumbent Martin Kennelly, were obligated to plead their qualifications. Trusting no one, not even the party chiefs who had selected him to be leader, Daley was not about to run any risks of someone's slipping him the double cross.

As he frequently said across the years, clenching his fists and striking a boxer's pose, a tough look on his face, in politics you've got to keep your hands out in front of you all the time. He remained in this defensive stance after his battle in the 1955 primary with Kennelly. Following his election as mayor, Jake Arvey confidently declared that now that Dick Daley had reached his long-cherished goal, he would quickly resign as party chairman. The two offices that Daley now held, Arvey said, were incompatible. At his first press conference in the mayor's office, Daley said he intended to resign the office of party chairman, although even then he had no intention of doing so.

In subsequent slatemaking sessions, in 1959, 1963, 1967, 1971—with Daley increasingly more secure as party chairman— it came to be axiomatic for Daley to be the organization's choice as candidate for mayor. So total was his control of Democratic party affairs in Chicago, so docile the raucous bunch of committeemen that he ruled, there was fear among the ward bosses that Daley, having had surgery in the summer of 1974, would decline to run in 1975. Indeed, some pleaded with him that he must remain as mayor.

If there had been any doubt of Daley's intentions of running again in 1975, there was none when he returned to Chicago from the Democratic party mini-convention in Kansas City, Missouri, in December of 1974. Praised and fussed over by even the party rebels in Kansas City, he came home with an inner glow to announce that he was willing once again to lead the troops to victory. Some of his committeemen openly wept in gratitude; others murmured that, well, he had no choice if he wanted to keep somebody else from getting a look at the books.

There was utterly no chance that the three Democrats who had had the bad judgment to declare against him could come even close to beating him in the February 25, 1975, primary; and it was irrational to expect that the Republicans, who at first couldn't persuade anyone to run as their candidate, had the remotest possibility of defeating him in the election of April 1. Daley's bid for a sixth four-year term was unassailable. So solid a favorite was Daley to win, it was only in deference to tradition that he bothered to campaign.

If ever a candidate for elective office had only a modest need of campaign funds, it was Richard J. Daley for Mayor in 1975. Yet, complying with a state law on campaign disclosure that took effect on January 1, 1975, Daley reported receiving total contributions of $588,307 after that date. He also reported having received $200,895 prior to January 1. Additionally, he reported receiving small contributions of $115,372 that he was not required to itemize. In total, Daley admitted in his first reports to a war chest of $904,574 to win a battle that was won before it was even begun, with still other contributions being disclosed later. Little note was taken that the Daley contribution reports identified Daley as both chairman and treasurer of the Richard J. Daley for Mayor Campaign Fund.

Money had poured in on Daley from many sources. The new requirement that those contributing more than $150 must be identified, with the amounts of their contributions specified, was witness that Daley had a broad base of support. Contractors doing business with the city of Chicago were credited in Daley's reports with having given him $183,438; almost $100,000 of this represented contributions from contractors who had received contracts running into the hundreds of millions of dollars on public works projects that ranged from subway work to laying concrete at O'Hare International Airport. Architectural firms, engineers, and lawyers who had received contracts from the Daley administration on a non-bid basis were also among the major contributors. So, also, were bankers, real estate operators, lawyers, and individuals who had been placed by Daley in high-income city jobs. Daley's report acknowledged that he had received $79,550 from labor unions, most of which had contracts that gave their city-employed members private industry wage scales, plus the holiday benefits provided for nonunion Daley administration workers.

A highly placed Democrat, running his eyes over the list of contributors that Daley had been willing to disclose, said, "This is like taking your piggy bank to Fort Knox"—meaning, of course, that it was superfluous to provide a candidate who had no chance of losing with such large sums of campaign funds. For purposes of comparison, it can be noted that at the time Daley was admitting to having received contributions of almost one million dollars, the Republicans were reporting total contributions of barely $40,000, of which $10,000 had been contributed by John Hoellen, the sole Republican alderman in the City Council—who had emerged, all others shunning the honor, as his party's candidate for mayor.

The three Democrats who dared to run against Daley in the primary were short of funds but heavy on criticism of his stewardship as they campaigned against him. Edward V. Hanrahan, the former state's attorney who had been dumped by the organization when his involvement in the unfortunate Black Panther raid of 1969 had made him a political liability, hammered at Daley on the law and order theme. His pitch was that, as mayor, he would "make Chicago the safest city in the nation"—the implication being that it wasn't too safe a city under Daley. State Senator Richard Newhouse, bridling at the sweetheart arrangements that the Daley administration had with the labor and construction people, kept emphasizing that when *he* was elected mayor, he intended "to bust up this cozy relationship now existing between the power structure, labor, and City Hall." William Singer, more knowledgeable about city administration than the other two Daley opponents, attacked the Mayor on a number of counts.

Aggressive, articulate, ambitious, Singer was the darling of the lake front and University of Chicago liberals. A young man, he had captured control of the 43rd Ward, ancient Paddy Bauler's old domain, prompting the now almost senile Bauler to abandon the city he had said was not ready for reform—old Paddy opting to spend his last years with a lady friend in Santa Fe, New Mexico. Having ousted Bauler, Singer had scrutinized the workings of Richard Daley, researching the mystery of how with favor and threat Daley had controlled the city.

Starting with a generous appropriation that the Daley budget provided for a City Council committee chaired by one of the old pals of His Honor the Mayor, Singer would seek to track the course of how a committee that rarely if ever did anything had managed to spend this money. When Governor Walker invited Alderman Singer to make a study of fiscal irresponsibility in the Chicago Board of Education, Singer grabbed at the chance— even though he knew that Walker was primarily interested in embarrassing Mayor Daley. There was widespread dislike of Singer among the organization Democrats, but there was fear of him, also. Tom Keane, the despotic City Council leader, had been continually in verbal conflict with Singer, but privately said that Billy was as well informed an alderman as he had ever seen.

A grinning Jewish boy, Singer was also long on chutzpah. Wise old troopers of the Democratic machine were wide-eyed, for example, when Singer set up a public-address system in the Civic Center Plaza, in the shadow of City Hall, and canted his psalm of deliverance from Daley's bondage. The hard-core Democratic workers marveled that Singer would dare to campaign in such a place, the courtyard of Daley's temple, and stoically listened as the young alderman cried out that they must shake off the chains that the machine had placed upon them. "You know and I know," he admonished the payrollers, "that you city workers are captives. Your jobs—keeping your jobs—depends upon how well you deliver the vote. Well, let me say that I believe you have the right to be free men and women. You have the right not to be forced to kick back part of your salary, which you are now compelled to do, to the Democratic machine."

There was some admiration among top-level Democrats for Singer's guts, but Daley took no notice of the Singer campaign. If it bothered Daley, he did not show it when Singer declared: "Richard Daley has disgraced himself and his city by creating the climate for the greatest collection of crooked politicians the city has ever seen!" There was no indication that Daley was offended when Singer made reference to Daley's remark, when he gave $2.9 million of public building insurance business to his son, that people could "kiss [his] ass" if they didn't like it. It didn't seem to bother Daley when Singer, expressing shock, declared: "Daley grew out of a political culture that regarded the public as chumps—so ignorant, so lazy, so uninformed that you could steal them blind and then have the arrogance to suggest that if they don't like it, they can kiss his backside."

Daley's campaign was reserved and sanitized. His appearances were limited to a few ward organization meetings, a few precinct worker luncheons, and other controlled situations where his exaggerated recital of his accomplishments was certain to be applauded. If the citizens he served paid any heed to what he was saying in his bid for another four-year term of office, they heard no reference to racial troubles, or financial crises in the school system, or his efforts to control the new Regional Transportation Authority that had been set up to resolve the public transit problems of the six northeastern counties of Illinois.

Daley appeared indifferent when the imprisoned federal judge Otto Kerner was hauled back to Chicago from the Federal Correctional Center in Lexington, Kentucky, to beg for freedom on grounds that he was dying of cancer.

Daley merely looked embarrassed when asked by reporters

why Tom Keane, under federal sentence for fleecing the city, had been observed sneaking into Daley's office via a little-used private door. The Mayor did not care to discuss the purpose of this visit, a few days prior to the primary, by this man who had brought disgrace upon himself and the city and who would soon be surrendering to serve five years of prison time.

Methodically mouthing his platitudes of how he had transformed his "hog butcher" city into nirvana, Daley abstained from comment when asked what he thought of the remark made in Washington, D. C., by national party chairman Robert Strauss that, personally, he would like to see the 1976 presidential nominating convention of the Democrats held in Chicago— "unless it appears that feuding between Mayor Daley and Governor Walker would embarrass the party."

Keeping his campaign in low gear, hewing to the line that Chicago was trouble-free and great because he had made it so, Daley stayed clear of all situations that might have provoked a challenge to his claims. His strategy was to skirt controversy.

He did not, for example, acknowledge that for six years no federal housing had been authorized in Chicago, because a federal judge, Richard B. Austin, had decreed that none could be funded until the Daley administration abandoned its policy of locating all such projects in the ghettos and other debilitated neighborhoods. Yet, speaking to the elderly residents of a housing project that had been built a decade earlier, Daley was able to speak of sharing a dream that he attributed to John Fitzgerald Kennedy: "It is our first duty to provide a decent home in a decent neighborhood for every American citizen."

Daley was dealing in drivel, so far as the reporters who had to cover his campaign were concerned. Neil Mehler, political editor of the *Chicago Tribune,* found himself not able to take any more of it. He wrote, as the campaign leading to the mayoral primary of February 25, 1975, came to its end: "For sheer demagoguery, we have not seen the likes of this campaigning." Chicago voters had been deluged, Mehler protested, with wild claims of great things accomplished. The boasting of wonderful things that Daley had done for the city, the promises of what the great Daley had in store for the underprivileged were, in Mehler's judgment, "just plain lies."

Lies or not, Daley scored an impressive victory, as witness the voter tabulations:

Daley: 463,623, or 58% of the total vote
Singer:.   234,629, or 29%
Newhouse: 63,489, or 8%
Hanrahan: 39,701, or 5%

The organization Democrats gloated that here again was proof that Daley was invincible. Daley had carried forty-seven of the fifty wards; Singer had carried three. There were signs of decay, however, in the primary tallies.

Voter disenchantment with Daley in the fifteen black wards of Chicago (the first indications that the blacks were turning against him having appeared when he ran in 1971) was now accelerated to the degree that the vote against Daley—the combined vote of Singer, Newhouse, and Hanrahan—was larger in some of these wards than the vote cast for Daley. The bloc of wards reverentially referred to by the professionals as the Automatic Eleven, a captive vote that up until the Martin Luther King assassination year of 1968 had invariably produced a plurality of at least 100,000 for all Democratic candidates, was now crumbling; the total vote of the Automatic Eleven was only 64,064 for Daley in 1975.

Conversely, as Daley's vote dwindled in the black wards, it blossomed in the white wards. In 1975 the overwhelming share of Daley's vote—357,000 of the total—came from fourteen all-white wards, in many of which he had had to fight for votes in his first three mayoral campaigns. Racially, Chicago's political mix was decidedly different in 1975 from what it had been when Daley was first elected mayor in 1955. Gone were the days when the late William Levi Dawson, peg-legged black congressman of the city's South Side, could turn out a plurality of 100,000 votes, and sometimes more than that, for the Democratic plantation boss from Bridgeport.

Failing to understand that the blacks were breaking free, Chicagoans scoffed when Senator Newhouse hailed his good showing in the 1975 primary as a victory. "This is not a defeat," he asserted. "We have shown that there is serious opposition to oppressive machine-dictated rule. Daley will not run again and the machine is dead without him." Whether the machine would be dead without Daley to run it was speculative; undeniably, the primary had pried loose the machine's grip on the ghetto vote.

The badly beaten Ed Hanrahan said, "The problem with Chicago is that everyone has a piece of it. When you share in corruption, you never want to do anything to stop it. There may be only forty thousand city jobs in Daley's control, but multiply them by a wife, a son, a cousin, or an aunt and then tell me, who wants to put Chicago on the square? Mayor Daley has won this election, but the people of Chicago have lost."

Billy Singer's liberals were desolate. Uniformly, they looked dour and some were weeping as their defeated young candidate stepped up to a headquarters microphone on primary night to address them. Smiling, Singer said, "I want to offer my congratulations to Mayor Daley." His followers groaned and shouted, "No, no!"—and Singer shrugged and stepped back, saying no more.

Some two thousand of the Democratic party faithful, plus the society buzzards who flap around when there is a scent of political meat, gathered in a big room at the Bismarck Hotel to await the arrival of Mayor Daley and his poker-faced family. There were food and booze aplenty; a band was blasting the only two numbers it seemed to know, "Chicago!" and "Happy Days Are Here Again!" Every woman in the place appeared eager to kiss the Mayor as he strode in, his bodyguards protecting him. Numerous men sought to shake his hand. The Shannon Rovers bagpipers from Daley's Bridgeport played their strident tunes, adding to the bedlam.

Daley had the look of a man who was loving every moment of this and it was with reluctance that he choked off the demonstration by indicating he would now speak. Network cameramen were hollering for lights and screaming at still photographers to quit blocking the line of sight. Sound men sat, earphones on, huddled near their boxes of equipment. On next morning's "To-day" program on NBC, and on all of the network news shows next evening, the nation would see and hear the great Mayor Daley of Chicago in his latest moment of glory.

What he said was: "It's a great night and all of you great men and women; it is a great victory for all. After this great victory and it's a tribute of all the work, everyone helping, the men and also the women and I'm grateful for everyone who worked so hard, for my programs as well as my performance. And after this great victory we must unite all the people of Chicago and unite everyone to make Chicago the greatest city in the world. And I think one says on a night like this, as I said the other times when I was elected and as I say again tonight, 'I shall embrace charity, love mercy, and walk humbly with my God.'"

The crowd cheered. The band played "Chicago!" The Shannon Rovers played "Garryowen," Daley's favorite tune, sounding similar to everything else in the Rovers' repertoire. Again the crowd cheered. The Mayor's clan gathered about him and out he walked. Harried bartenders were hard at work before the family reached the door. This was a night for serious drinking, and the drinks were free. With Daley on his way home, no one now cheered.

Next day, having bantered with the press, Chicago's $35,000-a-year Mayor flew off with his wife and some of his kids, first class, to Palm Springs, California. As he headed for holiday in a private residence at the Tennis Club—the guest of Harry Chaddick of Chicago, a real estate confidant who owned the place—Daley might have been pensive over the frightful erosion of his popularity in Chicago's black community, but he had the consolation that never had Republican fortunes in his city been so meager as now.

In a primary that had seen 800,000 votes cast for himself and his Democratic opponents, only 16,000 votes had been cast for the Republican nominee he would face in the April 1 election.

His Republican opponent, an obese fellow named John Hoellen, was running against him only because a candidate search committee that Hoellen headed had been unable to find anyone who would make the race and he had been reduced to selecting himself. Worse, in the aldermanic elections that are held in Chicago simultaneously with the mayoral primaries, Hoellen had been defeated in his bid for an eighth consecutive four-year term. For almost a quarter century, Daley had suffered Hoellen's disparagement and now—save for the pleasure of crushing his aggravator on April 1—Daley would be rid of him.

Predictably, the April 1 election was a disaster for the Republicans. Daley clobbered Hoellen in each of the fifty Chicago wards, getting 542,817 votes to Hoellen's 139,335. Daley had received a record seventy-eight percent of the votes that were cast. For the first time in one hundred years, not one Republican alderman had been elected to serve in City Council. With his fist on forty-seven of the fifty aldermen in the new council, only three independents having been elected, more than ever Richard Daley was free to do as he pleased. Additionally, the outgoing Council had voted to raise his wages from the $35,000 a year he had been receiving to $60,000—the argument for this being that Daley needed the money.

On rare occasions when politicians who knew Daley best poured themselves a drink and confidentially talked about him, the consensus was that he was not as gifted as admirers in the business community thought he was and not as bad as those who hated him would have others believe.

The politicians who knew him best thought it was unrealistic to credit Daley with creating a business climate that prospered. The judgment of those who had observed Daley closely over the years was that he had had nothing to do with the building boom of the sixties and seventies that saw the construction of such eye-popping structures as the John Hancock building, the Sears Tower, the Standard Oil building, Water Tower Place on North Michigan Avenue. . . .

Closer to the truth, the most qualified Daley watchers believed, was that most of the construction of this kind had been brought about by corporations whose stake in Chicago was so great—Sears, Roebuck, for example—that they had no option to relocate in some other city. The mighty structures that shot up in the heart of Chicago were the result of commitments made by chief executives of corporate giants that were locked into Chicago and had no choice but to stay put. Where, for example, could mighty Standard Oil of Indiana find a work force in its area, or have creature comforts to attract administrative staff, if it pulled out of Chicago?

The consensus of the informed politicians who discussed these things was that Daley had had the great fortune to be mayor of the city at a time when large corporations thought it necessary to expand. The politicians who talked about this found it wryly amusing that Daley, who had had nothing to do with decisions that ran into hundreds of millions of dollars, none of which was his money, proudly took credit for all that had been built.

Likewise, in constructing his political tickets, it was agreed by those who had been close to Daley that his first consideration was to select candidates who promised to be best for himself. Daley was not concerned that some of those he tapped to run for high office had no desire to do so. Secretary of State Michael J. Howlett, whose independence of Daley had created a veil of dislike between them, was one of those who preferred to take care of their own affairs and let Daley take care of his.

In 1968, after Governor Otto Kerner, Jr., had been moved up to a seat on the United States Circuit Court of Appeals, Howlett had sought endorsement from Daley to take Kerner's place as governor. In the obscure way that Daley had of juggling this kind of request, he not only expressed his opinion that the popular Howlett, strong with the voters Downstate, would make a fine candidate—he implied that he, Daley, would be quite in favor of having Howlett be the candidate. Subsequently, and characteristically, Daley slyly dropped his handkerchief behind someone else—former Lieutenant Governor Sam Shapiro of Downstate Kankakee, the acting governor, who had done Daley the service of filling up a dozen Circuit Court vacancies with Democratic party hacks. Howlett and Shapiro were friends and Mike had accepted the decision with good grace, even though he expected Sam to be defeated by Republican Richard B. Ogilvie, which he was.

Then, in 1972, with an upstart lawyer named Dan Walker having declared as an anti-Daley Democratic candidate to run against Ogilvie's bid for a second term, Howlett had another talk with Daley about his chances of being the organization candidate. Again, but in stronger terms than four years earlier, Daley said he thought Howlett would be a very good candidate. Daley stopped short of promising that he would run Howlett for governor, but he had said enough to impel Mike to go borrow $100,000 to get his campaign under way—the practice being that a candidate is expected to scratch up the seed money and repay it when the campaign is launched and the contributions start rolling in.

With Howlett on the hook for the hundred thousand and Daley aware that Mike was hiring office space and gathering staff, Daley walked out on him. Without so much as advance word to Howlett that there was a change of plans, without explanation of why he was opting for someone else, Daley announced that Paul Simon of Downstate Carbondale, Democratic lieutenant governor under the Republican Ogilvie, would be the Democratic candidate. Simon, regarded as almost too decent a man to be mixed up in politics, and politically naive, not only did not get elected governor—he was defeated in the Democratic primary by the anti-Daley independent, Dan Walker. Howlett was reelected in November with a massive vote as secretary of state.

Then, four years later, with the hated Walker winding up his four-year term and getting ready to run again in 1976, his eyes on the White House, there was talk in Democratic party circles that Mike Howlett was about to be tapped to run with Daley organization backing in the 1976 primary.

"I first heard of it," Howlett said, "from friends of mine who had been talked to by Daley's sons. The sons were urging these fellows to get me to talk to the Mayor, about running against Walker. I thanked these people for the invitation, but I didn't want any part of it. I made no moves. If Daley thought I'd be all that great as a governor, why didn't he think so in 1968 and 1972, for Cry sakes?

"Anyhow, I had to get together with Daley on various things from time to time and once, late in 1975, I went to his office to see him about something and he started talking about me running for governor. When I told him no, I wasn't interested, he dropped the subject. But he brought it up again, maybe three or four times, always when I was in the Mayor's office to talk to him about something else.

"He kept saying that he thought it would be a great opportunity for me. He said it had been one of his ambitions to have a Catholic elected governor of Illinois; he said we hadn't had one since 1912, I think it was, when we had a Governor Dunne. When I said I wasn't interested, Daley said I should recognize that I had a responsibility to see that Catholics had greater opportunities and that I should be a leader. He tried all kinds of arguments on me.

"I told him that I had told Jim Thompson, who was my friend and already running on the Republican side, that I would not run for governor. I told him that my friend Alan Dixon, the state treasurer, would never have declared on the Democratic side if I hadn't told him that I wasn't interested in the office. Daley just looked at me like I was crazy and said, 'That's nothing. What is a promise? How is a man supposed to make a promise, when he doesn't know the future, the opportunities?' He was something, that Daley.

"One day, in talking to him about something, he looks at me and says, 'Michael, who can tell? A fellow does a good job as governor, he may be considered for the White House.' Well, I laughed so hard I nearly choked. I couldn't help laughing and I could see that he didn't like it. Howlett is now in the White House? My God, I thought, this guy is crazy. But he started talking very seriously. 'No, no,' he says to me, 'you shouldn't laugh. You've got to consider that.' Then he goes on to tell me about a picture he has in his mind of me in a car going down Pennsylvania Avenue to be inaugurated. He said, 'She'd make a great first lady, Helen, your wife, liking everyone and knowing politics.' It was the damnedest thing I had ever heard in my life and I couldn't get out of his office quick enough. When I got home, I told my wife I had some big news for her. Helen looks at me like I am really nuts and she says, 'Daley said *that?* Glory be to God, the poor man is losing his mind!'

"Daley came back to the first lady business the next time I had a meeting with him. So I said, 'Listen: We're not talking about my wife being first lady in Washington; we're talking about her being first lady here in Illinois. I don't want that and she doesn't want it. My God, she doesn't even like the idea of living in Springfield. If I were governor, I'm not so sure I could get her to live in Springfield.' Quick as a flash, Daley says, 'Tell her she won't have to live in Springfield. You can always have a place up here in Chicago—a mansion in Chicago, to go with the mansion in Springfield.' He could be impossible, Daley could.

"Daley tried all kinds of things on me. It got so I hated to sit down and talk with him. One day, I just blew up. I got a little hot at him and said, 'Listen, I want to *live*. I don't want to go through that race for governor. I think that kind of a campaign could kill a fellow and there is no use in trying to talk me into it. Why should I get into a tough campaign, fighting a sonofabitch like that Walker, and maybe kill myself working for a job that I don't want?' Well, he put on a face like I had hit him and he shook his head like I was deserting him or something and then, real quietly, he says, 'Michael, they told me, running for mayor, the last time, if I did it I wouldn't live. When there is a duty to the party, you can't say no to the party.' So I just looked at him and said, 'Bullshit. I don't owe the party a goddamn thing.' And then I got up and got out.

"The next day I get a call from Bill Lynch, the federal judge that Daley made—his old law partner. Lynch was a great guy, you know, and didn't give a damn about Daley or anyone else. But he's laughing and he says he's got to have lunch with me. He's still laughing when we meet for lunch and as soon as he sits down he says, 'Mike, I'm ashamed of you. You have hurt Oscar's feelings.' Oscar, you know, that's how Lynch always referred to Daley—the way some of the fellows called him Geronimo, he called him Oscar. Well, I could see what had happened; I had hollered a little bit at Daley and he had complained about it to Lynch, and now here was Lynch going through the motions of passing the complaint on to me.

" 'Oscar says that you raised your voice to him,' Lynch says. 'He tells me that you slapped his desk and said the Democratic party could go to hell, for all that you cared. Oscar says he told you that he had run for mayor at great risk to himself, because the party needed him, and you told him the party had never done anything for you. He's upset, Oscar is.'

"Now, I hadn't told Daley half of what Lynch was saying I

told him. I had hollered at Daley, but, Christ, I was getting tired of hearing him talk about how I had to run. I actually did take a whack at his desk; I flattened my hand on it when I was talking to him. But I could see what Daley was doing; he was getting everybody who was a friend of mine to put the pressure on me.

"I went down to Lauderdale to get away from it, and out of nowhere a couple of the union guys come calling on me to say that I should agree to run. I couldn't pick up the phone without talking to the Teamster union guys, Bill Lee and Ray Schoessling and Louie Pieck. George Dunne called me and said that as president of the Cook County Board, he would appreciate it if I would reconsider. Then, Jack Touhy the state [Democratic party] chairman, who is a pretty good friend of mine, came up to my place in Long Beach, in Indiana, and asked if we could go for a drive; and on the drive Touhy came right out with it and said, 'Mike, you've got to do it for us. We can't stand to have Walker in there for another four years.' So I finally decided, what the hell, I'd do it."

The day following Howlett's conversation with Touhy, he had lunch with Daley at Democratic headquarters, then located in the LaSalle Hotel. He was not surprised to discover that, by way of making points for himself with Daley, Touhy had passed along word that Howlett had agreed to run. Daley was in a jubilant mood. The capture of Mike Howlett was now a fait accompli, as far as Daley was concerned. Aware that in dealing with Daley a prudent man should insist upon the spelling out of all the terms of an understanding, Howlett took a swig of iced tea and told Daley that there were some things they had better talk about.

"I told him I had gone through a long income tax investigation over the hundred thousand I had borrowed in 1971, when I thought I was being slated to run for governor in '72; I nearly fell out of my chair when Daley cut in to say, 'I made a mistake in '72; I should've run you. You would have beaten Walker, but I made a mistake.' I couldn't believe it; I never thought I would live long enough to hear Daley say he had made a mistake—about anything.

"Anyhow, I told him I wanted him to know that I had to claim the hundred thousand as personal income, because I had taken a tax deduction for the 12-percent interest that I had had to pay on the goddamned loan—writing out my personal checks for it. I didn't feel like telling Daley all of this, but you should come clean on everything when they are running you for office. So I told him and I told him that I had come out of it all right with the government and he cut in again to say that yeah, he knew I had come out of it all right. And I guess he probably did know it, because he was pretty good at keeping tabs on things like that—who was under investigation, how they were making out and all of that. But I wanted him to hear it from me, so that he couldn't holler later if Walker made a big stink about it and I looked bad, that I hadn't told him; you had to be very careful in dealing with Daley, or he'd leave you holding the bag if things went wrong.

"So then I told Daley about holding the job of vice-president at Sun Steel and why I was on the payroll—to keep peace in the Kaplan family, who were the owners. There was no big mystery about my Sun Steel connection; it was pretty well known that I had worked for the Kaplans for a long time—it was part of the public disclosure that I had to make as an elected official. Well, Daley broke in to say that he knew about Sun Steel and that it wasn't anything to worry about. I wasn't so sure it was nothing to worry about; Walker was going to go after me any way that he could. Daley should have known that; Walker went after Daley's kids, didn't he?"

Walker had indeed gone after Daley's kids, leaking to the press the startling story that the state license one son had received to engage in the insurance business and the state license that another son had received to deal in real estate were fraudulent—that the examinations they had taken had been doctored by examiners who were friendly to the Daleys. Information that the Daley kids had not been up to answering the examination questions and that the correct answers had been written in by the examiners, one of whom had subsequently been indicted and convicted for engaging in this rigging, could only have come from the Walker camp.

In blowing the whistle on the Daley kids, Walker incurred the lasting enmity of the Mayor. In Daley's elastic code of ethics, it was part of the game to make any sort of attack on your enemy, and uncivilized to be vicious toward his wife or members of his family. If a newspaper, on its own initiative, unearths and prints unsavory disclosures of a politician's family, you simply have to accept this. If your opponent feeds information to the newspapers, as Daley was certain that Walker had done, you can have nothing for such a man but loathing.

In politics, it is possible that the bitterest of enemies can be reconciled. Despite the personal way in which Walker had lashed at Daley during the 1972 gubernatorial campaign and thereafter, he could have been straightened out with Daley, as the politicians say, if he had been willing to recant and make an effort to get along with Daley, as Senator Adlai E. Stevenson III had done. Daley probably would have been willing to forgive Walker for just about anything—save for that business of mortifying his sons, which was unforgivable.

On the day he told Daley that he was willing to run as the Democratic organization's candidate for governor, Howlett saw how thoroughly Daley despised Walker. "I wanted to get it straight with him," Howlett said, "that if I was to be the candidate, I wanted something to say about who else would be on the state ticket. I had my own ideas of how a strong ticket should be put together, but Daley didn't want to talk about that. All he wanted to talk about as we had lunch was Walker.

"I said, 'Wait a minute; we've got to get this straightened out.' So he said, well, he figured we would run Neil Hartigan, the lieutenant governor, for my job as secretary of state, and state Senator Cecil Partee, for the black vote, would run with me as lieutenant governor, and my friend, Alan Dixon, the state treasurer, for comptroller. 'It'd be a great ticket,' Daley said. So I said, 'Like hell it will. It will tear us apart.' So he didn't like my saying that and he wanted to know what was wrong with it, his ticket? 'Everything,' I said.

"'The two top spots are governor and secretary of state; you can't have me and Hartigan, two Irish Catholics of Chicago, taking the two top spots; it'd kill us Downstate. Alan Dixon, who is not Catholic and very popular Downstate: he's been running for governor and he's a good friend of mine and we can't ask him to settle for comptroller. We've got to let Alan be secretary of state.' So Daley says what are we gonna do with Partee and Hartigan? 'I don't know,' I said; 'they'll have to settle for what's left. Cecil is a good friend of mine, but a black man running for lieutenant governor—it would kill us.'

"Well, we argue about it for a while and he tries to force me into taking his ticket; he keeps saying that he has had the experience and that he knows best. But I couldn't budge on this and so I came right out and told Daley, 'Listen, I don't want the goddamn job; I'm only running because everybody seems to want me. But if it's take it or leave it, your ticket, I'm out of it; I'm running again for secretary of state and you fellows can work out the rest of the ticket any way that suits you.' Well, I could see I was making Daley madder than a sonofabitch, but he could see he couldn't change me. So he says, 'All right. Here's the ticket'—and he ticks off the names: Howlett for governor, Hartigan for lieutenant governor, Dixon for secretary of state, Partee for attorney general. Daley was talking as if this ticket had been his idea right along; he kept saying it would be a great ticket, our best ticket.

"I didn't believe he could come around so fast; it was not the way he was. But he threw in Mike Bakalis for comptroller, saying that Bakalis was Downstate and that he had run real good in winning state superintendent of public instruction and that he'd help us get the school vote, and now we had a ticket. There was something funny about Daley giving up so easily: generally, with Daley, you had to do everything his way. But he seemed to be satisfied. So then we got down to talking about what he wanted to talk about."

What Daley wanted to talk about was Walker. Bad as it was for Walker having held the Daley kids up to scorn, almost as bad was the manner in which he had tried to undermine Daley's 1975 mayoral campaign. In an act of lese majesty, Walker had dispatched emissaries to his people in Chicago, when Daley was running for a sixth term in 1975, with a message: "You can be for Daley, if that's what you have to do, so long as you do it quietly and don't give the impression that Dan Walker is for Daley. But if you want to be against Daley, you can be out in the open against him, if you're careful not to let anybody know that Dan doesn't think much of him."

Double agents abounding in politics, and Daley having the best of networks, he quickly got word that Walker was eager to make him bleed a little, while pretending that he was not involved in a subtle defection. So, at a chance encounter between Walker and Daley, Walker approaching the Mayor with outstretched hand and an ingratiating smile, Daley shocked those who were present by whirling on Dan, snarling, "Say, I know what you're doing and let me tell you: I want you to be against me, out in the open. I want to keep you out in front where I can watch you." Looking embarrassed, Walker had flashed his Bugs Bunny grin and walked away.

To Howlett, Daley had said, "It's necessary to beat Walker in the primary and knock him out of there. He's too big a threat to the party. He's been against us, everybody in the party—me, everybody. Walker's got no feeling for the Democratic party and he doesn't belong to us. If we let him stay, he will wreck the party—he will eventually destroy the Democratic party in Illinois—and we can't let any man do that." If the price of getting Howlett to take the contract of eliminating Walker was acceptance of Howlett's choice of running mates, Daley apparently was willing to pay the price. Except—

In an unexpected maneuver at the meeting of party leaders where the 1976 state ticket was to be announced, Daley shocked Howlett. With the fifty Chicago committeemen, thirty township committeemen of suburban Cook County, and various county chairmen from Democratic strongholds Downstate in attendance at a private meeting, Daley attempted to make alterations in the slate of candidates that he and Howlett had agreed upon.

Moments prior to his announcement of who had been slated to run for what, he gave Howlett a peek at the slip of paper he held in his hand. Howlett was astounded to see that Daley had written down Cecil Partee's name as running for lieutenant governor, Neil Hartigan for secretary of state, and Alan Dixon for the minor office of comptroller. "Wait a minute!" said Howlett, and a heated discussion, carried on in whispers, ensued between them. "That's not the ticket that we agreed on," Howlett objected. Daley pursed his lips and sighed. Then, taking out a pen, he realigned the names of the candidates in accordance with the understanding he had had with Howlett.

"I never could figure out what made him do that," Howlett said. "I don't know whether he was trying to pull a fast one, thinking that I would go along with him, or whether he was slipping and just put the names down wrong or what. You never knew, dealing with Daley, what he was thinking. He wouldn't have promised Hartigan that he would run him for secretary of state, or promised Partee that he would be lieutenant governor; he didn't operate that way.

"I used to see fellows walk into Daley's office, you know, and talk to him about running for office. They'd walk out thinking that they had his support, when all he had said to them was something like, 'You'd be a good candidate and if you were the candidate we could support you. Go out and see what kind of support you can get.' To the uninitiated, that sounded like Daley was for them, when all he was saying was that if they went out and could show him that they could line up a lot of support, why, then he would like to talk to them about getting on the ticket. A lot of the candidates who wanted his support to run for president had this experience. A few of the smart ones could see that he wasn't promising anything, but a lot of them came away believing that Daley was really interested in them.

"A lot of these people running for president didn't care for Daley personally, I guess, but they all realized, as Bobby Kennedy had said, he could be the ball game. I know that [Jimmy] Carter tried to figure out Daley, and I think he decided that he wouldn't have a chance of getting Daley to endorse him until he showed Daley that he had picked up enough delegates to be taken seriously. If anybody puts together a list of Daley's mistakes, I think he should remember that Daley made a bad judgment on Carter's chances."

In many ways, Daley was inconsistent. Obsessed with the desire to smash the political career of Dan Walker, he did little to help Howlett accomplish the deed. He gave Howlett no campaign funds; he did not confide in Howlett his plans for getting out a big vote in the city of Chicago. And when—as Howlett had feared—Walker's people leaked damaging stories of Howlett's having paid income taxes on the $100,000 he had borrowed for his aborted gubernatorial campaign of 1972 (politicians not being obligated to pay income taxes on campaign contributions, *never* doing so), the implication being that Howlett had put this money in his own pocket; and when Walker's people planted with the press a question as to the propriety of Howlett's $15,000-a-year arrangement with Sun Steel, the implication being that Howlett was accepting some sort of bribe to do favors with automobile titles for the parent company, the mammoth M. S. Kaplan scrap dealer—the Mayor was a sphinx when questioned by reporters about the propriety of a secretary of state's having these involvements.

With Howlett doing a clumsy job of justifying his outside interests, Daley fled to Florida to escape the apparent scandal that was engulfing his candidate for governor and threatening to cost the Democrats the state of Illinois. On January 19, Daley interrupted his vacation to fly home for the opening of Mike Howlett's campaign headquarters. The presence of the party leader was obligatory, of course, and Daley made an appearance at the headquarters, mouthing platitudes of what a great governor Mike would be and what a great victory would be had in the March 16 primary. Alas for Daley, his flight from Miami's International Airport to Chicago had made him the center of attention.

Chicago newspaper reporters discovered that instead of spending $432 for first-class commercial tickets for himself, a bodyguard, and an aide, the mayor had chartered a jet that cost him $3,664. Additionally, the newspapers reported that Daley had been staying in a luxurious ranch house at the Ocean Reef club in Key Largo, its appointments including an enclosed swimming pool, that he had rented for the month.

As primary day neared, Daley stepped up his efforts to get out the vote. His multitude of precinct captains were brought in frequently to eat the chicken and green peas, or the overcooked beef and string beans almondine, and be harangued by Daley and by Howlett and the other candidates. Governor Walker had the advantage of the enormous patronage at his disposal and his own great energy; his television commercials, produced by David Garth of New York, were clever and slick. The attacks on Howlett's integrity had inflicted serious damage, and Howlett's fumbling efforts to defend himself had magnified, rather than pacified, widespread doubts about Howlett's honesty.

If the Walker campaign suffered from any weakness, it was—apart from having to overcome the vote that Howlett was certain to get from the Daley machine—political inexperience. If Howlett had a special strength, it was his ability to spot and cultivate those areas where he might do much better than predicted. Even so, the portly Howlett had been dirtied up by Walker's exploitation of Howlett's outside sources of income and damaged further by his own ill-tempered and bumbling efforts to rebut the charges.

Howlett was seething at Daley's indifference and unwillingness to defend him. But if the outside income issue was working to destroy Howlett, Walker was faltering under handicaps of his own: his quarrelsome inability to work productively with the state legislature; his record of having squandered the cash surplus that he had inherited from the previous administration; his shocking veto of $143 million of school aid—the veto mandated by a lack of state funds to pay the bill, but effectively dislocating school district budgets in all parts of Illinois. There was detectable disenchantment with Walker in the five collar counties that surround Cook. The cut in state aid for schools was provoking a discernible anti-Walker trend in the Downstate sectors where Walker had picked up the votes that got him elected four years earlier. In a pre-election statement, Walker conceded that he needed a heavy voter turnout to win. He didn't get it.

Howlett defeated Walker, 792,000 to 678,000. The Daley machine had failed to produce the 275,000 plurality in Chicago that Daley had promised; the margin was only 190,000, but this was accepted as the deciding factor in the March 16 primary, because Howlett's statewide plurality was 114,000. Privately, the professionals were agreed that Howlett won because he had cut deeply into Walker's vote in the Chicago suburbs and in the high population centers Downstate.

Although the first projections were that Howlett would get 54 percent of the vote and Walker 46 percent, and the returns consistently reflected these percentages, it was not until noontime the next day, March 17, that the bitter Dan Walker conceded defeat.

"The outcome didn't have anything to do with the issues," Walker maintained. "It was just a matter of their being able to get out the vote." He added a parting shot at Howlett's integrity, when asked if he would now support Howlett. He responded that there were "many unanswered questions" about Howlett. "Everyone in the media knows what these questions are. I believe these questions must be answered before I can make any decision."

A joyous Dick Daley had called Mike Howlett on election night to chortle that they had settled Dan Walker's hash. The *Chicago Tribune*'s headline said, *The real winner: Daley.*

March 17 was what the Irish would call a lovely day in Chicago. The skies were sunny and the temperatures were moderate and, at dawning, hundreds of floats were being assembled north of the river for the St. Patrick's Day parade. An exuberant Mayor Daley, a smiling Mike Howlett, and the extroverted Mickey Rooney, the performer, primping like a capricious leprechaun, all wearing green sashes with the inscription "Sons of St. Patrick," stepped off proudly, leading some seventy thousand marchers down State Street. Mobs of people, packed on the sidewalks, howled their support as the beaming Daley stepped along, looking as if he owned State Street, which in a sense he did.

Howlett had tried to engage Daley in serious talk of how they were going to handle the campaign against Jim Thompson, but Daley had no interest in talking about that. Howlett said, "I think it's going to be tough. Thompson didn't seem to know what he was doing at first, but they brought in some advisors from New York and they told him to get married, buy a dog, and take off forty pounds and he has done it all. Now, he is going to be tough."

Howlett was chagrined that Daley didn't care to talk about it. Changing the subject, Howlett said, "Carter did real good yesterday. What was it? Fifty percent of the vote for delegates? He's picking up steam." Daley grunted and then replied that they would have to wait and see about Carter; there were a lot of other good candidates, he said, and the nominating convention was a long way off. It was obvious to Howlett that Daley was not comfortable with the fact that the Carter vote in Illinois had been surprisingly strong.

"I think it bothered Daley to see Carter do this good," Howlett said later. "He hadn't paid much attention to Carter; I don't think he regarded Carter as his kind of guy. I think Daley was hoping that the nominee would be someone else, hoping Carter wouldn't do so good in the twenty-eight state primaries that hadn't been held yet. I think that Daley was hoping for a deadlocked convention, with nobody having enough delegates, so that he could swing the nomination to Adlai Stevenson."

Was Daley all that fond of Stevenson?

"Oh, hell, no; it was only that Stevenson running for president, being from Illinois, that was Daley's best bet for having a big place in the game. As for Daley liking Stevenson, personally, no, he didn't care all that much about Stevenson.

"With Daley, you know," Howlett said, "it was Daley who always came first; the other guy always came third with Daley, no matter who the other guy was."

Who came second?

"Nobody. That was Daley's percentage."

Chapter Three

"All you're looking for is any ordinary fellow who will be developed as President."

—Richard J. Daley

RICHARD DALEY FELL VICTIM to bad timing in pledging his Convention delegates to Jimmy Carter. In early May 1976, the Democratic nomination being within reach of the former governor of Georgia, Daley lacked the daring to pledge his votes to Carter. Instead of making the decisive and dramatic announcement of support that would have locked it up for Carter, Daley played coy and lost his chance to place Carter in his debt.

Daley conceded, early in May, that Carter "looks like a very outstanding candidate." He went further than this with a statement that Carter "has convinced people"—by reason of his state primary victories and displays of strength in such states as Illinois—"that he can win in the North." Carter was pleased, no doubt, to learn that the big chief had made this important concession that Carter could win in November, and not so pleased to hear that, in the same news conference, Daley the political genius had blundered—that Daley, raising his head in his defiant way, had declared, "I don't think anyone has it sewed up. The Convention isn't until July, and you'll see a lot of things happen between May and July."

Carter, aware that the nomination that seemed to be within

his grasp might be snatched away from him, could not have been pleased to learn that, in July, the Democratic bosses might contrive to choose some other "ordinary man" (Daley's phrase) as·their nominee. Having come so far in his quest for the nomination, the sensitive and suspicious former governor of Georgia had reason to be resentful toward Daley's sly suggestion that the nomination could slip away from him.

Carter might have been mystified by Daley's reluctance to admit that he looked to be a cinch to win nomination. To be sure, by mid-May Carter had fewer than half of the 1,505 convention votes he would require to lock up the nomination. California Governor Jerry Brown had jumped into the race as a youth-look candidate; die-hard loyalists were striving to create interest in the candidacy of the ebullient Hubert H. Humphrey; and the Morris K. Udall, Henry Jackson, George Wallace, and various other factions were continuing their pursuit of a miraculous turnabout that would propel them into contention with Carter. It was nonetheless apparent to seasoned observers, two months short of the New York City Convention, that there would be no catching the country-boy candidate from Plains, Georgia. Accordingly, Jimmy Carter was perplexed, if not annoyed, by Daley's stubborn refusal to embrace his candidacy and get the party's agonizing over with.

On May 25, having had another of his occasional long-distance phone calls with the Democratic patriarch of Chicago, Carter appeared to be making a plea for Daley's support, telling an interviewer, "I think Illinois Democrats would do very well in the general election with me on the ticket." What he was seeking was control of the almost one hundred Illinois delegates committed to Senator Adlai E. Stevenson III. Daley made no response—not the response that Carter wanted, at any rate.

"Our delegation will meet in New York in July and decide who their candidate will be," Daley said, when pressed on the matter of backing Carter.

On the same day, in a rousing speech in Los Angeles, Daley's principal political enemy, Illinois Governor Dan Walker, upstaged Daley by endorsing Carter. "Jimmy Carter has done what many people in the Democratic party have fought for and what

I have fought for over the last decade," thundered Walker. "Carter has the capacity to make America believe in itself again."

Daley was not the only member of the Old Guard to resist making an endorsement of Carter. It was around Daley, however, that the old pros in the party would be likely to gather to plot strategy aimed at forcing Carter to accept a vice-presidential candidate acceptable to them. Daley's choice was Senator Adlai Stevenson, but "Young Ad" had sniffed, when the question of being tapped for vice-president was put to him, that he wasn't "salivating" over the possibility that he might be chosen.

During the extended period of time when it had seemed that the race for the presidential nomination was wide open, and likely to wind up in a deadlock at the Convention, none of the active candidates able to nail down the 1,505 votes needed for nomination, Daley had fixed his mind on the idea of grabbing the prize for Stevenson. A liberal, a Northerner, and bearer of a well-known name, Young Ad had the attributes of a good compromise candidate. It was not until early June, with prominent Democrats elbowing each other to get identified as being declared for Carter, that Daley abandoned his dream.

Meeting City Hall reporters on the morning of Tuesday, June 8, Daley smugly said he had just spoken with Carter by telephone. "I said, 'Hello, Jim,' and we had a talk." Then, for the first time, Daley spoke as if he, finally, had decided that Carter was his man. "He started out months ago and entered into every contest in every state and he won 'em and he lost 'em, and, by God, you have to admire a guy like that."

Stubbornly, though, pressed as to whether he was not now endorsing Carter, Daley replied that most of the Illinois delegates were pledged to Stevenson and that they would remain so until they caucused in New York five weeks later. There was still the possibility, then, of a stop-Carter movement? Daley sizzled.

"We don't believe in stopping anybody. A lot of people stopped us. You know, in '72 they put us out"—and Daley's face clouded at the memory of his delegates being ejected from the Convention in Miami Beach.

A reporter asked Daley how he rated the belated effort of Senator Humphrey to maneuver the nomination for himself.

Never having liked Hubert, Daley dismissed Humphrey's chances. "I think anyone who doesn't stand the test shouldn't be running."

Wasn't it possible that Humphrey might be drafted at the Democratic National Convention? "Who said that he's the man now who should be knighted on a white horse to walk him into the Convention? I don't think anybody should be so honored, no matter who he is. And I don't think they will," he declared.

Moving back to the virtues of Carter, Daley said, "This man has fought in every primary. He's got something we need more of. He's got a religious tone in what he says, and maybe we should have a little more religion in the entire community.

"The man talks about true values. Why shouldn't we be sold on him? All of us recognize the violent and filthy movies, and the newspapers with all the mistresses on the first page stripped down to the waist! What are the kids going to do in the society that sees that around?"

Yet Daley steadfastly insisted, despite his approving references to Jimmy Carter's religiosity, that the Illinois delegation would continue to stand with Stevenson. The obvious explanation for Daley's holding back was that he was trying to arrive at a deal with Carter to lock Senator Stevenson into the vice-presidential spot. The irony of this was that Stevenson was making it difficult for Carter to choose him.

Less than a fortnight earlier, at Daley's fund-raising dinner for the Cook County Regular Democratic Organization, Young Ad had chided Carter for his failure to point out to the people of this nation the road over which he planned to lead them out of Republican party bondage. With a trace of petulance, Stevenson seemed to be annoyed at Carter's supposed failure to provide the American people with "new directions for their country." Daley, chin in his right hand, gazed at the young Senator impassively as a fat fox, as Stevenson declared: "The question is, who can govern?"

As always, there was some serious drinking at Daley's fund-raising dinner that May. It cost something on the order of $40,000 to set up the bars for a crowd of 5,500 at the Conrad Hilton Hotel in Richard J. Daley's Chicago, but—along with providing the faithful, the labor union people, the road builders, and other $100-per-plate contributors with a decent cut of filet mignon—it was part of the drill when you were seeking to raise $400,000 in one shot. A heavy meal on top of liquor produces listlessness, rather than euphoria, however, in a gathering of great size; and the noisy conversation that persisted at many of the tables at Daley's big fund raiser indicated that the guests had no interest in the barbs that Stevenson was directing at Jimmy Carter.

Unfortunately for Daley's planning, the Reverend James Wall of suburban Elmhurst was among those present, and it was safe to assume that, as chairman of the Carter organization in Illinois, Wall would carry to Carter a report that Young Adlai was taking shots at him. If, indeed, Stevenson harbored any hope that Carter would select him as his running mate, his speech at the Daley dinner was hardly the kind that would improve his chances of becoming Carter's vice-presidential choice.

Stopping short of an outright endorsement of Carter, in talking to reporters at City Hall on Tuesday morning, June 8, Daley said that if Carter did well in the Ohio primary on that day, he would assure himself of a first-ballot nomination at the New York Convention in July. Senator Humphrey, in Chicago for an appearance on the syndicated Phil Donahue television talk show, was apprised of this during a break in the taping at the WGN (*Chicago Tribune*) studios. Raising his eyes heavenward, Humphrey shook his head sadly and sighed, "Well, that does it." Next morning, Wednesday, June 9, Carter having won a landslide victory in Ohio, Daley could hold out no longer.

"The ball game is over," Daley said, alighting from his limousine on the LaSalle Street side of City Hall and confronting a crowd of reporters and television crews. Was he now prepared to vote for Carter? Yes, he was. Did this mean that the 100 delegates that he controlled, including the eighty-three pledged to Stevenson, would do likewise? Daley replied that, well, personally, he had only one vote and all he was saying was that he would cast it for Carter. His thoughts on Carter's chances of winning? "A man who went out and did what Jimmy Carter has done, there isn't any doubt about it."

In meeting with reporters later that day, Daley said he had had a phone conversation with Carter. He said he had mentioned to Carter that Adlai Stevenson would make a great running mate. Had Carter given him any sign that Stevenson would be selected as his running mate? Daley shook his head, wattles waving: "No. He didn't say anything."

In Washington, Stevenson called in reporters to announce that he was releasing his delegates—but this was several hours after Daley had released himself; and Tom Littlewood of the *Chicago Sun-Times'* Washington bureau reported that members of the Senator's staff had expressed "anguish" that the Mayor had spoken out before Stevenson had had a chance to say anything about surrendering his delegates. Stevenson also appeared to be annoyed that Daley was talking so enthusiastically about his being the vice-presidential nominee, that Daley had said, "I feel it would be a great ticket with Carter and Stevenson. It has identification all over the country. Everybody knows the name of Stevenson. Everybody knows the fine record of our Senator, and with a Southerner joining up with a Midwesterner—it would make a great ticket."

There was suspicion that Daley was up to his old tricks of trying to salvage something for himself out of a situation that he had miscalculated. But if Daley had ideas of maneuvering Carter into accepting Stevenson in return for getting his support, the thought of a deal was repugnant to Stevenson.

"I could never accept it, if it was part of an 'arrangement,'" said the Senator. Stevenson told reporters in Washington that Daley had assured him there had been no deal with Carter concerning the choice of Stevenson for vice-president, and added that rumors of such an agreement "have nothing to do with reality."

Stevenson disclosed that he had met with Carter on May 16, at Carter's request, and claimed that the subject of the vice-presidency had not come up in their conversation. "There is no need for him in his position to make any commitments for that office, or any office."

Privately, though, Nancy Stevenson, Adlai's personable wife, revealed that she and Carter's wife had been present during the socializing part of the May 16 meeting, and Nancy implied, by reason of the searching inquiry which Carter made into Stevenson's views—the surprising question, say, of "What would be your policies as president, if circumstances made it necessary for you to succeed me?"—that she thought Jimmy had asked for the meeting in connection with his search for a suitable running mate.

Indeed, in speaking to the reporters in Washington, Adlai said, "It is the most important decision that he will make in the next few months. It is his first major decision. Carter may be the first candidate in a long time who's had the luxury to spend time on this decision."

Was there wishful thinking in Senator Stevenson's references to the vice-presidential selection? He more or less denied this. "I don't lust for the vice-presidency. I don't seek it. I value my independence as a senator." Even so, one week later, Richard Daley declared, "I'm convinced we'll nominate and come out of New York with a great candidate for president, Jimmy Carter, and a great candidate for vice-president—and that'll be Adlai Stevenson." Daley made this prediction in Chicago's LaSalle Hotel at a June 16 dinner meeting of the Young Democrats of Illinois, adding a reference that he had been ousted from the 1972 National Convention in a credentials fight.

This time, he said, "there is no reason for putting anyone out. We want everyone in and everybody aboard." As the Young Democrats cheered, he was inspired to fabricate a bit of history. To support his ardent plea for party unity in 1976, he told his youthful audience that he could quote a famous saying of George Washington, when he was about to cross the Delaware. "You know what George Washington said to his soldiers? 'Let's all get in the boat'—that's what he said." The Young Democrats cheered.

In what appeared to be a sharp turnabout, Adlai Stevenson seemed to be trying to get his foot into Jimmy Carter's boat, two weeks later, on July 1, when both appeared at another of those $100-per-plate political dinners in Chicago. This time, in the now-familiar International Room of the Conrad Hilton—the crowd spilling over, as was frequently the case when the Chicago

Democrats were putting on the pressure to make money, into three other large rooms—the honoree-beneficiary was Michael J. Howlett, the Regular Organization candidate for governor, who had beaten the maverick incumbent, Dan Walker, in the March 16 primary in which Carter had made his first good showing in the delegate race.

Stevenson had been chosen to make the major address of the evening because Jimmy Carter, the probable presidential nominee, had accepted an invitation to be present. With Carter remaining uncommunicative regarding his thoughts on a running mate, the July 1 dinner provided Stevenson an opportunity to make a case for himself. It might safely be said that he took advantage of his chance by delivering perhaps the most effective speech he had ever made.

Speaking with a decisiveness for which he was not renowned, Adlai got started by telling Carter that Illinois would prove to be "the arsenal of Democratic victory in November." The enrapt Carter, head cocked and eyes fixed upon the surprisingly forceful Stevenson, beamed as the Senator cried, "We of the democracy of Illinois, Governor, plan to make you President!"

There followed, as if in outline of the campaign that the Illinois Democrats were calling upon him to wage, an acerbated litany of Nixon-Ford administration failure. "They've had seven years to prove themselves," the Senator declared. "They've proven themselves unfit. They gave us the greatest recession, the greatest depression, and the greatest inflation since the Civil War!" Daley was visibly in ecstasy. Guests close enough to the dais to hear him howled approval. Jimmy Carter's gaze remained fixed upon the speaker.

Immediately in advance of the Howlett dinner, a story had circulated that Daley had cornered the Senator and charged him to deliver the best speech of his life. Whether or not Daley had done this, there was not the slightest doubt that the Mayor was anxious for Adlai to make a strong impression upon Carter and thus further Daley's hope that Stevenson would emerge as the vice-presidential candidate.

Increasingly aware that his days as boss were running out and that there might not be another chance to play a key role in putting another Democrat whom he personally favored in the White House, Daley had seemed to harbor a dream that in a miraculous way it would be possible to get Young Adlai nominated. Carter's inexplicable success in the primaries had exploded the dream. It is, however, part of the liturgy of the Chicago Democrats that a man must put his sights on the prize target, working his way down as circumstances dictate. Carter having run off with the presidential nomination, the next target of opportunity for Daley's man was the *vice*-presidency. This met the operating principle of the Chicago Democrats that, whereas it is nice to get a full-course meal with vintage wines, if you can't have it you should at least try for a meaty sandwich, with a jug of good beer on the side.

With Daley hovering at his side like an unctuous maître d' who was not sure what would be forthcoming from the kitchen, Adlai knew down deep that it was hopeless to think he would be served the finest dish in the house. Personal pride dictated that he show disinterest, if not disdain, toward the vice-presidential sandwich that Daley was trying to deliver to him. But if Stevenson had no appetite for it, Daley seemed to be urging him to "eat the goddamn thing if you get it; it'll be *good* for us!" So there he was, Stevenson, at Howlett's dinner, pouring out his best speech to impress Jimmy Carter.

Those who paid attention to it were agreed that this was indeed as good a speech as Senator Stevenson could make. As luck would have it—a miscalculation, actually, on Daley's part— the press corps had deliberately been kept at a great distance from the speaker's table and so they heard only snatches of what the Senator was saying. It was a typical Daley trick to humiliate the press by ordering his security forces to keep the media people as far back as possible in the bus. Consequently, at the Howlett dinner the reporters assigned to travel with Carter simply did not hear the Stevenson speech that Daley wanted them to tell the nation about.

Reporters in the Carter entourage had been ordered to stand in a noisy doorway area quite distant from the speaker's table. Unable to hear Stevenson, they whispered a little joke to each other that Stevenson and Carter had shared a meal and that

Adlai had thereupon ordered an Alka-Seltzer which, like himself, didn't fizz. Otherwise, what mention they made of Adlai's good speech was that, as always, he had been halting and dull. Some even said that the speech had doomed any prospect he might have had to be chosen as Carter's running mate.

Adlai's speech, so different from what had been expected, in fact had hit the Howlett dinner crowd like a thunderbolt. The agenda unfortunately had required that Stevenson's moments in the spotlight must now devolve upon Mayor Daley, and it was the Senator's task to introduce the Mayor. The sum of his surrender of the spotlight came down to this: "You, Governor Carter, will never have a more loyal, steadfast friend than Mayor Daley." The audience leaped to their feet, applauding thunderously.

Jimmy Carter studied Daley as the Mayor gripped the lectern and grinned in acknowledgment of the applause. Daley was in no hurry to have it end. When, finally, it did—coming to the abrupt ending that was characteristic of these tributes to Daley—he spoke. This had been a busy evening and while he would go home to his place on South Lowe Avenue with the satisfaction of having received the most enthusiastic ovation, Daley could not regard himself as the top banana at this affair. Carter had yet to speak, and Daley, when he got around to it, would introduce him. Then Mike Howlett would speak; after all, this was Mike Howlett's dinner.

Daley had already been with Carter as the candidate was greeted by well-heeled Chicago area people who had been promoted into buying $500 tickets to shake hands with Jimmy Carter at a cocktail reception in the Blackstone Hotel. A fund raiser for himself had been Carter's price for showing up as the principal attraction at the Howlett dinner. It was reported, inaccurately, that Daley had arranged this. Many of those who were importuned to fork over the five hundred had indeed had their arms twisted by the Mayor's office, but credit for getting Carter to attend Howlett's dinner properly belonged to Hyman B. Raskin, who conceived the coup.

The sixty-five-year-old Hy Raskin had been brought in from retirement by his old pal Howlett to lend political expertise to

Mike's campaign. Not since Raskin, hand-in-hand with the late Joseph P. Kennedy, had engineered the nomination and election of John F. Kennedy in 1960 had Raskin had an active role in politics. A lawyer, Raskin had prospered as a consequence of President Kennedy's having been at pains to let it be known that Raskin had his ear. Now he was back in the game—putting aside the tennis racket that he swung so gracelessly and the more somnolent pleasures of retirement in Palm Springs, California.

There had been grumbling, actually, in the high circles of the Daley organization that Mike Howlett had run an inept primary campaign, even though he had decisively defeated the organization's archenemy Dan Walker. Some upper-echelon people had complained to Daley that Howlett had pretty much sat on his ass in the primary and that *they* were the ones who produced the victory over Walker. So it appeared helpful that he had brought in Raskin.

Raskin's political pedigree traced back to Jake Arvey. He was acknowledged to be the technician who had structured Jack Kennedy's success in the state primaries of 1960—especially in the Western states. But Raskin was never considered to be a Daley man, and Daley's people were suspicious of him as they were suspicious of anyone who was not in Daley's control—including their candidate for governor, Mike Howlett. Even so, Raskin had the instinct to recognize and capitalize on any special situation that he came upon in handling a campaign; he proved this by getting Jimmy Carter to fly up to Chicago from Plains, Georgia, for the Howlett dinner.

Carter's campaign manager, Hamilton Jordan, had demurred when Raskin called him. Jordan agreed that a large Democratic dinner in Chicago would be a great pre-convention showcase for Carter, with the Democratic party pooh-bah, Richard J. Daley, seated at his side. But Jordan drawled an objection that the Carter camp was short of cash and that Jimmy had to be used in fund raisers that would do Jimmy some financial good.

"How much money are we talking about?" asked Raskin. "We can do something for Carter, but give me a figure of what would satisfy you."

When Hamilton Jordan hesitantly suggested that they would

like to get $100,000 out of the deal, the knowledgeable Raskin replied that, well, this was supposed to be a dinner to raise money for the Howlett campaign—but would Jordan settle for a guarantee of $50,000? Hamilton Jordan's voice was smooth as southern syrup as he quickly responded that it would be mighty fine to come out of Chicago with fifty. They firmed the deal on Raskin's guarantee that Carter would get fifty and possibly more than fifty.

Daley was elated when Howlett telephoned to say that Carter would show up for the July 1 dinner. When Howlett explained that Raskin had made a commitment to raise $50,000 for Carter—"There will have to be a cocktail party or reception, or something like that"—Howlett expected that Daley would say responsibility for Carter's reception would be Mike's problem. Instead, Daley replied that *he* would "take care of that."

There were two reasons for Daley's quick response. First of all, a special affair for Carter afforded Daley an opportunity to elbow his way to the side of a potential president who seemingly had been trying to keep a polite distance from him. Second, the audacious Governor Walker had stolen a march on Daley with an earlier announcement that *he* was planning a fund raiser for Carter, even though Carter had scrubbed the idea, wisely avoiding involvement in the feud between Walker and Daley. A reception for Carter—with Daley getting credit for the financial success it was certain to be—afforded a fine chance to give Walker a lesson in one-upmanship.

It was decided to have a $500-per-person cocktail party for Carter in the Blackstone Hotel, across the street from the Conrad Hilton. This would be the prelude to Howlett's dinner. The room was filling up with cheerful givers, most of whom had been pressured by Daley's aides into forking over the 500 clams (some, indeed, receiving the "request" personally from His Honor the Mayor, an invitation that could not prudently be refused), and the liquor was flowing at about the time that Mayor Daley was greeting the ex-governor of Georgia at Chicago-O'Hare International Airport. Confident that there was a sufficient stack of $500 checks on hand to assure that Carter would get the $50,000 that he wanted, Daley was likewise getting the exposure with Carter that he devoutly wanted.

In a rare gesture of party unity, Daley had accorded the Reverend James Wall, Carter's campaign manager in Illinois, the privilege of riding out to O'Hare in Daley's official limousine. They were not a synergistic pair, Daley and Wall—the Irish Catholic big-city boss and the Baptist minister from the suburbs—and it irked Daley that Reverend Wall had his nose farther into Carter's tent than he did; yet the rule is that a smart politician accommodates circumstances to make the best of an unfavorable situation, and Daley made an effort in the drive to the airport to treat Wall as an equal, aware now that Carter trusted Wall's counsel.

It had been, for example, Reverend Wall who had advised Carter to place a phone call to Mayor Daley after each of the state primaries. Asked to confirm this, Wall had said, "Yes, Jimmy Carter keeps in touch with him. We agreed that the thing to do was keep in touch with the Mayor personally after each primary was over." In every instance, although Wall avoided mention of this, Carter had made a futile plea for Daley's support. Daley, a vain man, had to be gratified that the leading candidate for the presidential nomination was eager for his blessing; yet, he had carefully avoided making a commitment to Carter—just as Carter coolly declined to promise Daley that, when nominated, he would choose Adlai Stevenson as the vice-presidential candidate.

Reverend Wall had been an advocate of patience with Daley, during the intransigent period when Daley's endorsement could have been had on a straight trade for Carter's acceptance of Stevenson. Reverend Wall was new to the game of politics, just as other Carter Baptists throughout the nation were sight-learning the rules. Wall had, however, an intuitive sense of what was advisable and possible, and even professional Democrats in Illinois voiced grudging admiration of the manner in which Wall had used his church, gathering his fellow Baptists into an effective political force, to help produce a surprisingly good delegate vote for Carter in the March 16 primary, Carter getting fifty-nine to Stevenson's eighty-three—Hubert Humphrey winning only four and George Wallace only three, with fourteen uncommitted delegates rounding out the Illinois delegate count of 163. Congressman Paul Simon (D., Carbondale)—the Daley organi-

zation candidate for governor in 1972, who had been creamed in
the primary of that year by Dan Walker—observed that Carter's
Illinois campaign had been "extremely adroit," which was a decent compliment, considering that Simon was attempting to pro-
mote the candidacy of Senator Humphrey.

With a sizable bloc of the state's delegates, Reverend Wall had
been in a position to contest Daley's claim on chairmanship of
the delegation. It was not in the Carter plan, however, to precip-
itate useless quarrels that could impede his advance toward his
goal. Consequently, following the primary of March 16, Reverend Wall made a point of urging the selection of Mayor Daley
to be chairman of the Illinois delegation.

After hearing of this, Wall's willingness to let him head the
delegation, Daley confided to John Touhy, chairman of the Illinois Democrats, "This Wall is all right"—meaning that Daley
could coexist with a fellow who seemed to know his place.
Touhy, who had been weaned on politics, his father having been
Democratic boss of Chicago's West Side even prior to the reign
of Anton J. Cermak in the 1930s, had acknowledged Daley's
compliment to Reverend Wall with a nod of agreement; the politically astute Jack Touhy had learned at an early age that, in
politics, you avoid comment if you can.

Touhy knew very well that Daley was concerned that even
though the Democratic party was in good position to elect a
president, he, Daley, was in jeopardy of being left out of it.
Touhy had recognized for many weeks that Carter would sweep
to a first-ballot nomination at the Democratic Convention and
believed that Daley was exercising poor judgment in fencing
with a Jimmy Carter who was every bit as shrewd as Daley.
Touhy knew that Daley had waited too long to line up with
Carter; not even the last remaining big-city political boss of the
nation was in a position to bargain, having held off so long that
his support was no longer urgently needed.

The Illinois Democrats' strategy had been to keep the numerous presidential aspirants at a distance from Daley, until such
time as a likely candidate would emerge in the state primaries.
As each of the potential nominees sought to make a connection
with Daley, Touhy and Howlett would offer to hold a breakfast

for him in Springfield with the county chairmen. This had begun with a breakfast for Jimmy Carter in September of 1975, when hardly any of the organization people had even heard of him.

It might not strike an outsider as a matter of great value or consequence, being introduced by Secretary of State Howlett as "my friend and an outstanding candidate for president." But this was a chance for Carter to speak with county chairmen who get out the vote, many of whom would be delegates to the nominating convention, and the candidate had been delighted to have this chance. Carter, a veritable stranger in Illinois, had been genuinely grateful to Howlett. Little wonder that he seemed to think that winning the favor of Mayor Daley should be the next objective. Little wonder that he was perplexed by Daley's apparent disinterest in his plans for winning a decisive number of convention delegates, Daley limiting himself to offering him only boilerplate encouragement.

This is how a big-city boss plays the game, of course: encourage them all, while keeping a distance from them. A big-city boss can hurt himself, however, if he fails to respond to such evidence as a candidate's consistently good performance in the primaries—and Daley had held off too long on Carter. By the night of July 1, as the Mayor headed back to downtown Chicago from O'Hare Airport, Jimmy Carter in the car with him and Reverend Wall, it should have been clear to Daley that Carter did not now need *him,* so much as *he* needed Carter.

This was to be a night of glory for Daley, sharing attention with the man who already was regarded as certain to be nominated and elected president. National Democratic chairman Robert S. Strauss, hardly a shy violet, had called to say that he was flying in to be with Carter at Mike Howlett's dinner. John Cardinal Cody had accepted an invitation from Howlett to deliver the invocation. Starting with the cocktail party for Carter at the Blackstone, this promised to be a big evening. The Democrats had a winner!

The $500-per-person crowd had consumed several drinks by the time Carter was escorted into the Blackstone by His Honor the Mayor. The guests were noisy and rude, crowding up to get a look at the guest of honor. If there had been a plan to have

Daley stand with Carter in a receiving line, Carter scrubbed that by moving into the crowd on his own—leaving Daley engulfed in well-wishers who wanted him to know that they had paid their $500 and that they were there.

Disassociated from Carter by those who wanted to have a word with the Mayor and detained him, Daley was quickly not in a position to judge what kind of impression the drawling man with the fixed smile, thick lips, green-gray eyes, and casual set of his wheat-colored hair was making on those who were shaking his hand. Smiling uninterruptedly, worming his way through the crowd, introducing himself over and over again as, "I'm Jimmy Carter and I'm runnin' for president," the candidate was continuously on the move. He acted, as one observer said, "as if every time he shook hands, he was picking off a vote to put in his pocket."

Several important people in the Chicago financial community were disappointed in Carter's studied refusal to respond to their direct questions regarding his views on investment credits, tax philosophy, and international matters, such as continuation of détente with the Soviet Union. "He smiled as if he had not paid the slightest attention to what it was I had asked him," a financier with a close advisory connection to Daley later complained. "It was a waste of time to be there, and I would not have been there if the Mayor had not insisted upon it," the financier said.

But if some of the $500 contributors were negative in their first face-to-face appraisal of an uncommunicative man who appeared to be destined to lead the nation, both Carter and Daley were pleased by the sizable number of people who had turned out to get a look at the candidate in ascendancy—even though, when Carter stepped to a microphone to say a few words to this crowd, the unabated laughter and conversation in the room were embarrassing evidence that there was little interest on the part of this throng in hearing whatever it was that this sing-song candidate was trying to say.

The situation was markedly different from this, when Carter, Daley, Howlett, Strauss, Touhy, and the state candidates of the party crossed the street and made their entrance into the International Room of the Conrad Hilton. The applause was quite loud as the $100-per-plate diners struggled to their feet, in what appeared to be a genuine demonstration of approval. Carter grinned broadly and Daley looked to be beside himself with joy. It was undoubtedly true, as Hy Raskin observed later, that in all of his travels, Carter had not seen such an outpouring of Democrats as this.

The food was expensive—the bill was $65,000 for 4,000-plus dinners—but the dignitaries didn't get a chance to do more than taste it. The principals at the speaker's table were hardly seated before Jack Touhy had them on their feet again, leading them to the three other packed dining rooms, Carter, Howlett, and Daley speaking briefly in each room. They were hardly back in the International Room before Touhy got the introductions going. If it is the custom for Carter's Southern Baptists to suffer through tediously prolonged services, it is standard practice for the Chicago Democrats to reach early adjournment of their big fundraising dinners.

The Reverend James M. Wall was introduced, following some preliminary remarks by national party chairman Robert S. Strauss—who apparently had shown up to quiet rumors that Carter did not think much of him and planned to dispense with Strauss as chairman at an early date. Predictably, Strauss paid lavish compliments to Daley and Carter and provoked a slight response with a statement that there was not "a state race anywhere in the United States more important than Mike Howlett's election here in Illinois." The crowd had expected Strauss to say something of this kind, but they perked up when Wall succeeded him at the rostrum.

Reverend Wall had been frequently short on charity in his references to Richard J. Daley. A liberal who had sniped at Daley's resistance to change, Wall had been regarded as allied with the anti-Dick Daley forces of Governor Walker. Speaking now to a Daley who had been converted to the Carter side, Wall declared, "Mayor Daley is preeminent among Democrats in the United States who realize that politics is a process of give-and-take, adjustment and strong leadership." Wall made a ministerial gesture toward Daley, the Mayor, hands folded on his belly, gazing at him with the look of a man who agrees that this praise of him is well deserved, and said, "Mr. Daley is Mr. Democrat." He went on to say, "Mayor Daley is the man who triggered the landslide that will give us the next president of the United States." It was interesting that Daley joined in the applause.

It was utter nonsense that Daley had set off a landslide for Jimmy Carter. But this was a night that was intended, in part, to smooth out wrinkles in party unity and Carter smiled approvingly as his man, Wall, poured extravagant compliments upon Daley. When Senator Stevenson, who was the speaker following Wall, continued the theme of praising Daley for his loyalty and friendship for Carter, the candidate-to-be continued to smile as he nodded his agreement. While he looked to be surprised that Daley was being rocked in a cradle of exaggerated praise, Carter's attitude seemed to be that this would redound to his benefit at both the Convention and the election in November.

Daley was the next speaker and he got a thunderous ovation, Carter widening his eyes in apparent surprise that this old bird would be so warmly received. When, finally, the applause suddenly stopped and the crowd sat down, Daley got right to the business of introducing his state candidates. He also introduced their wives, after presenting his own wife, Sis, who briefly stood at her place at a front table, located directly to the side of where Daley, Howlett, and Carter were seated.

Daley carried off in quick style his part of the program. He got in his usual bromidic references to the greatness of the Democrats and he made an impassioned plea for party unity. He carefully avoided any reference to Governor Walker, Carter's old Navy friend, who had boycotted both the $500 Carter reception and the $100 Howlett dinner—the lesson for Carter, in Daley's ignoring a sticky situation, being that the safest course is to look the other way when there is trouble within the Democratic fold.

Carter was aware of the intraparty bickering in Illinois. Indeed, Walker had come dangerously close to getting Carter into disfavor with Daley, with a plan to hold a fund-raising breakfast for Carter in Chicago. Carter extricated himself, with a message to Walker that he would not be available to attend Walker's breakfast. But it hardly escaped the attention of Reverend Wall that no Walker people were named to the committee that Daley had then set up to peddle the $500 tickets to the Carter cocktail party. Jody Powell, Carter's press secretary, replied when asked about this that the Carter organization didn't want anyone excluded from an active role in the Carter campaign. Even so, there was concern in the Carter camp that Boss Daley was moving in to take over Carter's campaign in Illinois. The suspicion was that he would try to force upon Carter the selection of Adlai Stevenson for vice-president as the quid pro quo. The suspicion was reinforced on Carter's July 1 visit to Chicago.

The frequency with which Carter was asked about Stevenson's chances, as he moved about among the 300 or 400 guests at his Blackstone Hotel cocktail party, did not escape notice of Carter staff people who had clung to his side and heard the question being asked. Later, one Carter aide speculated that this was a contrived thing on Daley's part. Time and again, Carter was asked for his opinion on whether Senator Stevenson would make him a good running mate. Repeatedly, never blinking and never losing his smile, Carter had replied: "Your Senator Stevenson is well qualified to be vice-president or president, and he's one of those I have considered carefully."

Stevenson was not present for the cocktail party; his plane from Washington was late and he barely arrived in time to march in with the 125 others who took seats at the speaker's table at Mike Howlett's dinner. He might have been appalled to learn that Daley-connected people were pushing his cause; besides, he had a good speech in his pocket in which he had a strong sales pitch of his own. Carter aides could only speculate on why Stevenson was not attending the cocktail party; it had the mark of intrigue of the sort that Daley supposedly was noted for. If the absence of Governor Walker was to be interpreted as proof that Daley was in control of the Democratic party in Illinois, what did it mean—influential friends of Daley pressuring Carter for word of Stevenson's chances—when Stevenson himself was not there?

Carter got a standing ovation when Daley introduced him at the Mike Howlett dinner, but the applause was markedly less in intensity and duration than Daley had received. As if guided by an applause meter, Carter immediately launched into surprisingly extravagant praise of the Mayor. His staff had done its homework, and Carter revealed himself to be a man who was capable of retaining in his mind the essentials of a briefing—starting off with a statement that Daley had won reelection to a sixth four-year term in 1975 with an incredible 78 percent of the vote. "It's almost a miracle," Carter asserted, in his prayerful voice, "but then you have a miraculous man." Carter stepped back from the microphones and raised his head in approval as cheers filled the room.

The dinner crowd was uniformly attentive, hanging on Carter's every word. Daley pursed his lips and nodded solemnly as the speaker said that Daley's endorsement on June 9 had been the turning point in his long quest for the Democratic nomination. Carter said that he had telephoned Mayor Daley early on June 9, the morning after his victory in the Ohio primary, and asked Daley if there was anything that he might say about the endorsement at a press conference he was to hold later that day in Plains, Georgia. In his staccato style, he said:

"Mayor Daley told me, 'You can tell them [the reporters at Plains]: I'm for you. I'm committed to you and I'll try to help you get delegates in Illinois,'" waves of laughter greeting Carter's report that Daley said he would "try" to get him delegates in Illinois. *Try?*

Getting back on track, Carter continued: "Mayor Daley said he would help me in every way. Mayor Daley said: 'And I'll help you become president. Is that enough?' And I said, 'Yes, sir!'" Waves of laughter filled the International Room; Carter was telling this audience that *he* knew who was boss, and they loved it.

Perhaps now, many thought, with this good start, Carter would come out with an endorsement, or near endorsement, of Adlai Stevenson for vice-president. A statement of this kind would have electrified this crowd; with Adlai sitting there at Carter's side, balding, angular, and looking unpressed in his narrow-lapeled Brooks Brothers suit, button-down collar, and old-school tie, the scene was right for a surprise preview of what would be the big moment of the Democratic Convention, two weeks hence. Only, Jimmy Carter is not a politician who makes a move until his schedule calls for him to make it. So instead of saying the slightest thing about Adlai's winding up on his ticket, Carter almost deliberately worked the house for laughs.

He kidded himself about his smile, explaining that now he had something to smile for. He made a reference to someone from Plains, Georgia, having an idea that it was possible to be elected president. Then, with a quick compliment to Stevenson's admirable service in the United States Senate, Carter got serious and said, "I am here tonight to pay homage to Mike Howlett. I am confident that Mike Howlett will give Illinois tough, competent management." The crowd applauded, Daley seeming to be pounding his palms together louder than anyone else. Then, in his cute little way, Carter chided Daley—as if taunting him to explain where Daley had been when Carter desperately needed him.

"A year ago," Carter said, "I had only one friend in Illinois: Mike Howlett. There was no one else. No one knew who I was or cared to help me. And then Mike Howlett called me and asked me if I'd like to come to Springfield and meet some Democratic county chairmen. I was eager for that chance. And pleased. And grateful. I *had* a friend in Illinois."

Howlett gazed like a happy bear upon the speaker. Daley, looking serious, threw an accusing look at poker-faced Jack Touhy. No friend in Illinois, except Howlett? Nobody ready to do anything for Carter, except Howlett?

"Mike invited all of the Downstate chairmen to my breakfast. I had the list of those who had been invited and I had a girl at a table, outside the breakfast room, to check off the names of those who showed up. One of the chairmen went up to this girl and asked what she was doing. 'Oh,' she said, 'Governor Carter wants to have the names of the county chairmen who attend the breakfast, so that he can keep in contact with them.' The fellow smiled in a friendly way at this girl and said, 'Miss, they have all been invited here by our good friend, Mike Howlett, so you don't have to sit there and keep a list. They will *all* show up.'"

The Howlett dinner audience loved it, only a few of them suspecting that the presidential candidate who had calculated the importance of every step he had taken in his perilous journey down the primary trail, who had measured everything he uttered, had now deftly tossed a barb at Daley. Daley knew.

The big fund-raising dinner came almost to an anti-climax with a short speech by the guest of honor, Howlett. He pledged to give Illinois a "new chance"—to reduce unemployment, improve the quality of education, to increase aid to the handicapped: all of the usual things. Then, quickly, a rabbi was brought forth to give the closing prayer, and the vast crowd raced for the exits.

In a 16th-floor suite, half an hour later, Hy Raskin sipped a soft drink and said: "You should have seen Hamilton Jordan's face when I told him we were sending them back to Plains, Georgia, with a hundred and fifty thousand from the cocktail party!"

There had been almost 4,500 paying guests at Howlett's dinner—and the last 1,000 places had been sold when announcement had been made that Carter, who had the nomination in his pocket, would be one of the principal speakers.

The only person of any consequence who had not shown up was John Cardinal Cody, the Roman Catholic archbishop of Chicago, who had agreed to give the invocation. Nobody seemed to know, or care, why Cody had sent a monsignor to take his place.

Mike Howlett had ducked out to his apartment at 535 North Michigan Avenue. Jack Touhy had gone home to his condominium in Lake Point Towers. The Carter people, who might have stayed the night in Chicago, opted to head back at once for Plains, Georgia. Richard J. Daley the Mayor and Mrs. Daley, looking tired and appearing to want privacy as they walked down the main staircase to Daley's limousine, which was waiting at the Michigan Avenue entrance of the hotel, silently got into the car and headed for their brick bungalow on South Lowe Avenue.

Next morning, over poached eggs and coffee, Daley met at Democratic headquarters in the LaSalle Hotel with state chairman Jack Touhy.

"It was a nice affair," Touhy said.

"Well," Daley replied, "we showed 'em how you do it with your organization."

"I think Carter was surprised at the size of the crowd," Touhy responded.

Daley pursed his lips. He ran his fingers over his jowls. "He didn't have to say that, what he said. Howlett isn't the only friend he had in Illinois. He doesn't seem to know, this Carter, how it is done in politics—with so many candidates runnin' for the nomination and that early. It was last year, you know, Howlett's breakfast for him. He didn't have to say, last night, Howlett was the only friend he had in Illinois; we are all supportin' him; he knows that. So why did he have to say it, about Howlett?"

Stoically, not knowing what he might reply, Daley obviously believing that Jimmy Carter had deliberately put him down at Mike Howlett's dinner, Jack Touhy said nothing.

Chapter Four

*"It's great to be back. It is like I have
never been away."*

—Richard J. Daley

THE BEST-KNOWN BIG-CITY BOSS to attend the 1976 Democratic
National Convention felt sadly out of place. The form letter that
Richard Daley received from national chairman Robert S.
Strauss, as did all delegates and alternates, promised, "From the
minute you get out of your plane, train, bus, or car, you and the
members of your delegation will feel right at home."

By prearrangement, a limousine was waiting when Daley and
Mrs. Daley, their number two daughter, Mary Carol Vanecko, and
their sons, Richie, Michael, John, and William, stepped off the
American Airlines 727 at La Guardia. A slight, no-nonsense veteran
of the New York City Police Department was at the wheel, tersely
announcing to Daley's security people that he would be on twenty-
four-hour call; with a man who could pass through police lines with
a mere glance at the officers who were turning most other traffic
away, *this* was "just like at home"—but little else was.

The Illinois delegates had been left to their own devices in
booking flights to the New York Convention; no chartered plane
this time—no affectation of unity and camaraderie, none of that
rally-round-the-chief this time. Not only did Secretary of State
Michael Howlett, the Democratic candidate for governor of Illi-

nois, fly into New York with his group on a different flight from that of Daley; the same was true of state Democratic chairman John Touhy, and the power structure of the Daley organization—the Alderman Edward Burkes, the Alderman Edward Vrdolyaks, the Alderman Vito Marzullos, plus the top-ranking ward committeemen—all of whom customarily traveled to conventions in a pack.

Customarily, the Chicago Democrats clung to their leader as pilot fish cling to the back of a shark. Only in getting to the abortive nominating convention of 1972, when the rebellious followers of Senator George McGovern were striving to shut them out, Daley remaining secluded in his summer place at Grand Beach, Michigan, had the Chicago crowd been obligated to fend for themselves.

In 1960, they had flown off joyously to Los Angeles, as spirited troops march into battle—an invasion force securing a beachhead for the Chief, Daley making the journey leisurely in a private car of the Santa Fe—to help Daley secure the nomination of John F. Kennedy. In 1964, with a light heart, they had descended en masse upon Atlantic City, confident that even though there was nothing that the Mayor wanted from Lyndon B. Johnson at this Convention, the Mayor would hold an honored place at the council table, that the President would be solicitous, that Daley would get advance word on what Johnson's pleasure would be in the selection of a vice-president, a professional courtesy that would be denied him by Jimmy Carter and his provincial Georgia crowd.

A readjustment of professional courtesies, a discarding of special considerations for those who had figured prominently in Democratic party affairs and who traditionally had been accorded gracious treatment, was to be a hallmark of the Carter takeover; Carter's crowd, from almost the moment that it had control of enough delegates to assure Carter's nomination, was notably unencumbered by any obligation to be indulgent toward the Old Guard. Not only was Daley to be casually bypassed; the survivors of the John F. Kennedy and Lyndon B. Johnson reigns were to have no privileges at the New York Convention. The battle cry of the Carter crowd, from the moment that the nomination had been captured, was "Ask not what we can do for you, but rather ask what you can do for us." Daley might have been disheartened to discover this, but he had followed the same principle in exercising authority—and still did.

In conventions past, Daley had been flanked by such self-assured millionaire Democrats as Thomas E. Keane and Jacob M. Arvey. Daley had always appeared to be ill at ease to have these two professionals at his side, as if fearful that he would be upstaged, although both Keane and Arvey seemingly had always been at pains not to impinge upon his authority as delegation chairman. Now, in New York, when Daley could have used advice and counsel, he stood alone and was reduced to coping as best he could with his fear that he was being disfranchised by a new party leadership that did not seem to regard him as necessary in the election of a president. Confronted by evidence that he was to be an outsider, not only was Daley separated from two men who had had much to do with furthering his own career; he had created a situation of permanent estrangement with both of them.

It is doubtful that the eighty-year-old Jake Arvey would have attended the 1976 Convention in his old role of delegate-at-large if he had been invited by Daley to be there. With a half century of high-level service in the Democratic party—successor to Mayor Edward J. Kelly as chairman of the Chicago organization, a man who might have blocked Richard J. Daley's path to power, friend of Franklin D. Roosevelt and Harry S. Truman, longtime member of the Democratic National Committee—Arvey was entitled to some show of deference on Daley's part; he got none. And whereas it might be true that a thick hide is prerequisite to survival in politics, Arvey was visibly offended by Daley's indifference.

Contacted by a reporter as he sat secluded in his law office in Chicago, as to why he was not attending the Convention in New York, Arvey quietly replied, "Daley did not invite me. At my age, I would have refused the invitation; the task of nominating a Democratic party candidate for president now belongs in younger hands. At my age, I would have refused an invitation to be a delegate, but the fact is that Daley did not invite me. He didn't give me the chance to refuse—he simply didn't ask me."

Tom Keane, of course, was in prision. Found guilty in federal court of having deceptively used his control of city council to grab title to tax-delinquent real estate that he subsequently resold at huge profits, Keane was now serving a five-year term. Another former Chicago alderman, Paul T. Wigoda, who had served time in the same institution for income tax evasion, on a $50,000 zoning case shakedown, had recently come home on parole with word that Keane was having a difficult time in making an adjustment. Still protesting that he had been indicted, tried, convicted, and sentenced for a malfeasance conspiracy that grew out of a more loathsome conspiracy by the administration of President Richard M. Nixon to "get" the Richard J. Daley machine, Keane was losing his eyesight and was in a state of despair that no one on the outside was doing anything to ease the burden on his wife, Adeline. Wigoda did not say Keane believed that Daley had abandoned "Addie," but those who heard Wigoda's dour report inferred that the imprisoned number two man of the Daley machine had come to the sad conclusion that Daley had decided that Keane would be of no further use to him and that Addie could shift for herself.

Elected in 1975 to succeed Tom as alderman of the once-powerful 31st Ward of Chicago, Mrs. Keane had timidly taken her place in the City Council—rarely having anything to say, consistently voting in favor of whatever it might be that the Daley administration might propose. In the primary of March 16, 1976, she had been elected as a Senator Stevenson delegate to the Democratic Convention; in the frequent telephone calls that Keane was permitted to make from prison, he had urged her to do this, assuming that it would give Addie pleasure to participate in the nominating process. Additionally, the Keanes had spent many happy holidays in New York, with entrée by reason of Tom's connections to choice seats in theaters, restaurants, and clubs, and he thought it would be nice for Addie to relive some of these experiences. Judging from the sadness that seemed to engulf Addie, walking through the Waldorf lobby to board a bus for Madison Square Garden, toying with a fork in the hotel coffee shop where she took her meals during the Convention,

Tom had miscalculated; it was with only a haunting sense of déjà vu that Mrs. Thomas E. Keane endured convention week, 1976, in New York City.

Accustomed during Tom's day to special treatment at every turn, traveling first-class all the way, with limousine service on a twenty-four-hour basis at both ends ot the journey and the best of accommodations in New York, diminutive Adeline Keane had gone from her home to Chicago-O'Hare Airport by taxicab; she had no airline personnel fluttering about her as she sat in a corner of the boarding lounge, waiting for the New York flight to be called; and it was not in the first-class cabin but rather in a center seat of the coach section that she made the journey to New York.

There had been no one, other than a grandson who traveled with her, to assist her with the handling of the luggage at either end of the trip; she traveled light, in contrast to the packs of luggage that she had taken along when traveling with Tom, but Mrs. Keane looked forlorn, actually, as she stood with a suitcase and a garment bag on the 49th Street side of the Waldorf, where she had debarked from an airport bus, waiting for a bellhop to get her into the hotel and through the unfamiliar drill of registering. She was settling, this trip, for a tiny room in this place where, oh, so many times, she and Tom had occupied the most expensive of the suites. Through all of this, there was not the slightest sign that her husband's old associate Richard Daley had any interest in her peace of mind or comfort.

During the time that Tom Keane had been on trial, and during the many months of appeals before his incarceration, Daley had made a point of being nice to the Keanes. Not only were the Keanes placed in seats of honor at various functions controlled by Daley, but the Mayor also took every opportunity to proclaim his faith in Tom's integrity, denouncing in harsh Bridgeport tones the federal government's practice under District Attorney James R. Thompson of prosecuting Daley machine people on the basis of having secured damaging testimony from fellow conspirators who had been granted total immunity. Daley had many times declared his admiration and loyalty toward his good friends Tom and Adeline Keane. Yet, at the New York

Convention in 1976, with Tom in prison and Addie in need of at least a gesture of solicitude, Daley had ignored her.

Consequently, it might be said that Daley had no equitable reason for complaint in New York that the Carter crowd was treating him in the same disinterested fashion.

Richard Daley's arrival at the Waldorf Astoria had caused a momentary flutter. Springing from his limousine with an agility that surprised the doormen and the bellhops, Daley had marched into the hotel from the garage entrance, had got into an elevator with Sis and his boys and his bodyguards, and had been taken directly to the 26th floor and led to his suite by an assistant manager—All quite businesslike, these arrangements for his arrival.

There were flowers in the suite and baskets of fruit; in short order, a large cart of liquor, beer, soft drinks, ice, and snacks—peanuts and pretzels—would be coming through the door; and there was a flurry of activity as the baggage was brought in, the bellboys stealing a look at Daley as they scurried to get the Daley entourage's bags sorted out into the bedrooms where they belonged. Daley sat in an overstuffed chair, hands on the armrests, his well-shod feet planted on the carpeted floor, as if waiting for the activity to subside. Daley had the appearance of a potentate, keeping his own counsel as he awaited phone calls of welcome from those who had maneuvered themselves into control of Democratic party affairs—chairman Strauss, candidate Carter, and all others who might go through the ritual of being solicitous, in at least a pretense of creating party harmony.

For the most part, Daley was to wait in vain, if he thought that his role at this Convention was to be that of preeminent elder statesman, to whom all others would come, beseeching him to counsel them on how to gird for battle with the Republicans. He might have had some vague suspicion that his sphere of influence was limited now to the matter of delivering the vote of Illinois (if, indeed, he could succeed in doing that), but it had become increasingly apparent that Boss Daley was now a latter-day Jim Farley or Averell Harriman whose inventiveness had been largely discounted.

On the eve of the 1976 Convention, Daley sported medals

won in old battles; yet, like every aged general who has outlived his time as a member of the high command, he was now more of a symbol of campaigns to be waged and glory to be won than a strategist whose advice was considered to be vital to victory. The prevailing opinion among the new leadership was that, while Daley's backing in Illinois was still something to be sought, Daley's kind of politics was swiftly becoming old hat.

Daley's mind seemed to be fixed on a desire to remain on stage, even in a diminished role, until the final curtain. He was not comfortable with the prospect of Jimmy Carter, a stranger to the Democratic hierarchy, taking over the political party of the people. What hold did anyone have on this Carter? Where would you be if he got to be elected and you had to go to him for help in the multimillion-dollar funding of a rapid transit subway, or a billion-dollar expressway?

Well, you take what you get in politics and make the best of it; this had always been Daley's rule of survival. If you had private reservations about the reliability of a Jimmy Carter, you adjusted to the idea that, inexplicably, he has emerged and you expressed a confidence that he would mature in high office and "do the right thing"; this was Daley's way. "Remember Harry Truman in 1945," Daley had said; "a lot of people were very critical and now he is written up as one of the greatest presidents. Every man who holds the office, President, the office does a lot of things to him."

Every man who holds the office, Big-City Mayor, the office does a lot of things to him, also. Especially, the Big-City Mayor who gets elected to six consecutive four-year terms and who comes to be regarded by business people and politicians in all other major cities as an administrator without equal—granted that many held him to be devoid of conscience when it came to stealing votes that were needed to get his man elected. As he sat with his thoughts in a suite of the Waldorf Astoria on the eve of the 1976 Democratic Convention, Daley would have had to acknowledge, if he could be honest with himself, that his problems in Chicago were multiplying beyond any capacity he had to resolve them, and—insofar as exerting influence on the election of a president was concerned—his last taste of glory dated back to the election of Lyndon B. Johnson in 1964, and he had not had a crumb of success to feed upon since that time. Indeed, it had been Daley's inability to carry Illinois for Hubert Humphrey in 1968 and for George McGovern in 1972 that had ripped away any credentials he might have had as a maker of kings. Little wonder, therefore, that he had shied away from Jimmy Carter as yet another political pauper, holding off so long that he lost any claim he might have had as trusted adviser to the nominee-to-be.

Some areas of the press seemed to think that Daley had cleverly worked a coup in conceding the nomination of Carter more than a month in advance of the Convention, rather than waiting to make his move, building up an attitude of suspense, until the dramatic moments when nominations were in order, the eyes of all delegates upon him, as was his practice. But if some political writers misread Daley's cunning, others did not.

In a June 10 "think piece" under a Washington, D.C., dateline, the *Chicago Tribune* had measured the question, "How did a fresh new face like Carter manage to win over a shrewd old pro like Daley?" The *Tribune* report dismissed the suspicion expressed in some sectors of the media that Daley had struck a deal with Carter, trading his support for Carter's promise to name Adlai Stevenson for vice-president. "You don't cut a deal for the vice-presidency with only 85 [sic] delegates," the *Tribune* observed.

The *Tribune* quoted Congressman Paul Simon as saying that Carter had been extremely adroit in his Illinois campaign, staying clear of the Chicago wards in his search for delegates and supporting the Mayor for head of the Illinois delegation. The *Tribune* quoted "a Daley watcher," not otherwise identified, as saying, "The two men are very similar. They are both wheeler-dealers, but they are both religious, too. There's not a great deal of difference between a church-going pious Catholic like Daley and a church-going pious Baptist like Carter." Closer to the truth of why Daley had scrambled to get aboard Carter's bandwagon was the *Tribune*'s conclusion: "The old man just didn't want to get left behind this time."

At the organizing caucus of the Illinois delegates in a crowded, overly warm private dining room of the Waldorf Astoria on Sunday afternoon, July 11, Daley rose from his seat at the head table and in a tone of defiance declared, "I'm happy to be a part of it." The delegates, who had just routinely confirmed his nomination to be chairman, politely applauded.

The caucus had been called to order by Jack Touhy, Democratic chairman of Illinois, but it was apparent from Touhy's solicitude for the Reverend James M. Wall, Carter's man, that the pretense of leadership was being bestowed upon Daley simply because it was politically expedient for the Carter camp to avoid making waves that could wash away Democratic votes on November 2. The situation was clearly understood by the Daley forces; after all, Reverend Wall had been a delegate to the 1972 Convention in Miami Beach, pledged to Senator McGovern. The Daley crowd was loath to forget or forgive its enemies.

"To me, the Democratic party in Illinois will be united, solidified, and cemented by the nomination of Jimmy Carter!" the newly elected delegation chairman declared. Reverend Wall smiled. "We're gonna have one state and one people," Daley went on, "and I am confident, I know it, we will have a great victory for Jimmy Carter and Mike Howlett in November."

Touhy, standing up as Daley sat down, thereupon called for nominations for vice-chairman. By agreement, there were to be two; in a voice vote, the winner was Ms. Suellen Johnson of Wheaton, a Republican Party stronghold located some forty miles west of Chicago. Bearing this with a grin, Daley wriggled in his chair to move it over and make room for the placement of a chair alongside him for Ms. Johnson. He joined in the applause as the young woman made her way to the head table, applauding vigorously when she stepped to the microphones at Touhy's matter-of-fact invitation and gave a two-word acceptance speech, "Thank you." Women's lib had cracked the chauvinistic barrier of Daley's inner circle, but this girl had sense enough to know, by God, that it wasn't her place to stand up there and give them one of those equal-rights harangues.

Mixed in with all this were brief seconding speeches by a few of the Chicago ward bosses, including one by the seventy-seven-year-old Vito Marzullo, who had served in Chicago's City Council since 1955, the year that Richard J. Daley had first been elected mayor. A few of the delegates from scattered parts of Illinois also were called upon to speak, including a large, visibly happy black woman from downstate Champaign—Anna Wall Scott, a schoolteacher, new to politics—who finished up her pro-Carter homily by suddenly stooping down to Daley and, catching him unawares, planted a fat-lipped kiss on his cheek.

The room filled with genuine laughter as Daley got to his feet, looking the fool as he sought to wipe away the kiss with the back of a hand. Daley sensed that the joke was on him and he appeared to resent it. As if anxious to divert attention from himself, he leaned toward the microphones and unexpectedly blurted, "The chair now recognizes a great congressman from Chicago, Danny Rostenkowski."

Rostenkowski, who had been seated inconspicuously with the other Illinois delegates, was surprised to be introduced. Senior among the Democratic congressmen from Illinois since canny old John Kluczynski had died, Rostenkowski had succeeded to Klu's place as Daley's man in Washington. But whereas "Johnny Klu"—who enjoyed little of his twenty-eight years in Washington, aside from a weekly poker game with such chums as Richard M. Nixon—tolerantly did his best to satisfy without challenge whatever it might be that Daley wanted him to do, Rostenkowski was prone to dispute Daley's wisdom in certain areas and he had quickly been replaced as Daley's man in Congress by a hard-working and docile Chicago congressman named Frank Annunzio, who knew how to take orders. Rostenkowski, in short, was surprised to be called upon to speak and, as he said later, he had not the slightest idea what it was that Daley wanted him to say.

Lacking any cues, and inspired perhaps by a friendly handshake from Adlai Stevenson as he got to the head table, Rostenkowski paid verbal tribute to the great Mayor of Chicago and then offered a motion that the Illinois delegation unanimously petition Jimmy Carter that it was the desire of the delegation that Senator Stevenson be chosen for vice-president. Daley sat blinking, as if wishing that *he* had thought of doing this, as the motion was seconded and carried with no detectable dissent. So then it was Stevenson who had to speak.

The delegates had been getting edgy before Rostenkowski had awakened them with his pitch for Adlai. What had been planned as a brief caucus had been dragging along, the temperature in the room was climbing, and the afternoon was slipping away. Daley was to be host at a reception in the Empire Room following the caucus, and everyone was expected to make an appearance at this. Then, there were other parties to attend and other places to be. The caucus had proved to be tediously prolonged and likely to drag on with more speeches, now that Rostenkowski was proposing Young Adlai for vice-president. Of course, Carter himself had disclosed that Adlai was one of the six potential choices he had in mind for a running mate; further, it had been disclosed that prior to the opening of the Convention at Madison Square Garden next day, Carter had planned a private discussion in his suite at the Americana Hotel with the Senator.

"I am looking forward with great interest, frankly, to a meeting tomorrow afternoon with Governor Carter. I am but one of a number of men, all exceedingly well qualified, who are under consideration. Come what may, in the next four days, I will support wholeheartedly whoever Governor Carter's choice might be." So spoke Senator Stevenson.

There were outcries from the delegation that he, Stevenson, was the candidate that Illinois wanted. Stevenson smiled in that wan way of his and said, "Well, whatever my own role is, I simply want to do all in my power to assure victory in November for Jimmy Carter—and Mike Howlett." Nodding toward Daley, Stevenson went back to his seat. Shortly, to the visible relief of all present, the caucus was adjourned.

Mary Mullen, Daley's longtime personal secretary, who had served for years as madam factotum of Democratic headquarters in Chicago, her blue Irish eyes continually on patrol, her photographic memory snatching every detail of any conversation or development that struck her as significant, or of some possible value in the future, was already on station outside the entrance of the Empire Room, ready to take note of everyone who filed into Daley's reception for the Illinois delegates.

Ms. Mullen was not located there to screen the guests with

any thought of denying entrance to anyone; she smiled, for example, when the dour *Chicago Daily News* columnist Mike Royko, chronically outraged critic of the Daley Democrats' venality, slouched by to eat Daley's food and drink his booze. Her function was not to deny anyone Daley's hospitality, but rather to send word to Daley by one of the party functionaries nearby that so-and-so had arrived. It was standard practice for Daley to avoid surprise.

As usual at Democratic conventions, Daley's reception was an extravagant affair. In making arrangements with the food and beverage people, it was a point of Irish pride with Mary Mullen to make certain that the guests would snack on excellent fare and that an adequate number of bars would be set up; it was part of the scheme of the Daley organization's hospitality to overestimate what might be needed to satisfy the guests' bellies and throats. Expensive, to be sure, the tab with gratuities running into thousands of dollars—most hotels nationwide insisting upon prepayment of at least 60 percent of the bill before uncorking the first bottle of whiskey or deveining a solitary shrimp.

Not in all the years of Daley's long reign as chairman of Cook County Democrats had money been a problem. Most of the Illinois delegates to the New York Convention, and the alternates and the camp followers, had to provide their own funds for travel, living expenses, and entertainment, but the organization paid the bills for the Daley family, the administrative people, the press agents, security people, the Mary Mullens, and so on. Perhaps the Internal Revenue Service might be curious about political funds' being used to cover personal expenses, but this had long been the practice—the war chests of political organizations providing perquisites of extraordinary kind: wardrobe expenditures, personal entertainment expenses, generous sums of pocket money, and so on.

It would be difficult, if not impossible, to identify the source of the thousands of dollars that it cost to transport the Daley gang to New York and back to Chicago again at the Convention's conclusion, providing the lot with expensive shelter, extravagant food, theater tickets, the purchase of gifts, and whatnot. A careful audit, if one could be had, most likely would trace all of this money back to the net profit from the May 19 fund-raising dinner of the Chicago and Cook County Democratic organizations—Honorable Richard J. Daley, chairman of both.

Something on the order of 6,000 persons paid $100 per plate to attend this affair—ward bosses, city payrollers, union stiffs, contractors, and so on—the crowd so large that it spilled over into thirteen dining rooms. In a campaign disclosure report that was later filed with the county clerk, in compliance with state law, the Daley organization admitted to a net profit of $619,903.

In addition to the ticket sales, the coffers bulged with contributions from an interesting assortment of people:

• The 11th Ward Regular Democratic Organization, Daley's base, contributed $17,000.

• The even more lowly 25th Ward Organization, headed by Vito Marzullo: $8,000.

• The Chicago ward superintendents, who supervise the collection of garbage and the removal of snow—supposedly selected, these men, by civil service examination, but actually dependent upon approval of Democratic ward committeemen in getting these choice $32,000-per-year patronage jobs: $5,000.

The document of disclosure filed with the county clerk provided even more interesting clues as to how The City That Works actually works:

• Brighton-Krug Contractors contributed $4,000 to the May 19 dinner. This firm was one of two general contractors on construction of the $38-million parking garage at the City of Chicago's O'Hare International Airport and had received over $2 million in city contracts for runway repair, street resurfacing, and other public works projects. (On September 21, 1976, incidentally, Thomas J. Bowler, fifty-three-year-old partner in Brighton-Krug, a good friend of Daley, was indicted by a federal grand jury in Chicago on nine counts of income tax evasion in the years 1970, 1971, and 1972, the indictments charging that he understated both his personal and corporate income. In the three-year period, Bowler reported total adjusted personal gross income of $580,590 and total corporate income of $1,444,553, not bad for a Bridgeport man who had started as a tuckpointer, the government charging that the true totals would be "substantially in excess" of what he reported.)

• Another $4,000 was contributed to the Democratic dinner jointly by two old family construction firms, Kenny Construction Co. and Paschen Contractors, Inc., both firms having received multimillion-dollar contracts from the city—including a co-general contract on a $37-million share in the rebuilding of the fire-gutted McCormick Place on Chicago's lakefront, and such projects as $7 million in demolition and sewer construction.

• Paxton Landfill Corp. made a $3,000 contribution to the May 19 dinner. For six years, Paxton had operated the city's only sanitary landfill. In 1975, after contributing $8,000 to Mayor Daley's reelection campaign and the Democrats of Chicago, Paxton won a controversial rezoning case that permitted it to expand its landfill operation to sixty acres of Chicago's South Side.

• A. A. Electric Supply Co. contributed $3,000 to the May 19 dinner. This firm had been awarded a $10.5-million city contract to replace 82,500 mercury-vapor streetlights with high-intensity sodium-vapor lights.

• James and Thomas Flanagan were listed in the Democrats' document of disclosure as having contributed $1,000 each to the May 19 dinner. The brothers Flanagan were principals in the Heil & Heil Inc. insurance agency of Evanston, which had had the wisdom to employ one of Mayor Daley's sons, John, and which subsequently received on the arbitrary order of Daley more than $3 million in city of Chicago insurance business—the revered Mayor shocking some of his true believers by angrily declaring, when the insurance deal became public knowledge, that a man is entitled to help his sons and that those who did not like his doing so could "kiss my ass."

• There was even evidence, in the Democrats' report on the May 19 contributors, that political donations are nonpartisan. Lester B. Knight & Associates, for example, which had been awarded an architectural contract to design a $16-million criminal courts office building for Cook County, was listed as having given $2,000 to the May 19 dinner. This was the same Lester B. Knight who had previously been identified as a $50,000 contributor to the Richard M. Nixon reelection campaign fund in 1972, this contribution having been made four months after his firm had been awarded a $1-million federal contract.

Standing midway between a huge buffet table and a bar at the far end of the Empire Room, two of his sons and his security people nearby, Richard Daley looked bored as the flow of guests at his reception swirled around him. Numerous people stopped to pay their respects and Daley was cordial in the brief conversations he had with those who worked their way through the crowd to shake his hand. He appeared neither animated nor vibrant. He would visibly brighten up when an occasional important senator or governor was escorted to his presence for a brief exchange, but the general impression he created was that the parade had somehow passed him by; at least, that he was no longer up there in front, helping to lead it.

This first day in New York had been a commonplace day. Up early, Daley had shaved and bathed and had breakfast in his suite. Then he and Sis and two of the boys had gone over to mass in St. Patrick's Cathedral, drawing hardly a glance from the other worshipers. Back at the Waldorf, Daley had decided to visit Madison Square Garden and see for himself what kind of location the Illinois delegation had been assigned; his boys went with him in the limousine. Having had his look, largely ignored by the network engineers and trade-union people who were putting the Convention floor in order for the first session next evening, Daley had taken the escalators back to the ground level and made the long walk to the Seventh Avenue entrance of the Garden. Moving his legs in the wooden-soldier manner that was characteristic of him, he had climbed into the limousine; his driver had parked in a privileged spot in front of the Garden, and then driven him back to the hotel. It wasn't much that he had done, but he had nothing else to occupy his attention.

There were phone calls to be answered, back at the hotel. Daley was told that, during the Convention, his car would have ramp privileges and he would be driven into Madison Square Garden. Daley fretted that no one at the National Committee had bothered to ask him what he needed in the way of gallery seats; chairman Strauss had included a couple of floor passes, in allocating credentials for the Illinois delegates and alternates, and Daley had taken possession of these for his boys, but he had no seats to hand out to influential Chicago people who had come to New York with confidence that the Boss, Dick Daley, would get them into the Convention.

This was not the first convention in which the national chairman had given Daley the back of his hand. The late Paul Butler had done this in Los Angeles in 1960, making a point of assigning Illinois a third-rate hotel, placing the Illinois delegation at the very rear of the Los Angeles Arena, across the aisle from Texas, which was also out of favor with Butler, and ignoring Daley's need for gallery tickets. It happened, though, in 1960, that William McFetridge, Daley's trusted connection with organized labor and a member of the hierarchy of the Flat Janitors' union, was a delegate. Becoming aware of the ticket problem, McFetridge cunningly had resolved it by having members of his union's Los Angeles local open up a family entrance for the Chicago crowd at the rear of the convention hall; by merely presenting McFetridge's business card, on which he had written his signature, anyone could get in or out at will, and, once inside, make his way into the gallery and take any seat that happened to be unoccupied. There was consternation at the Los Angeles Convention among those with valid tickets who were denied a place to sit down because someone else, courtesy Bill McFetridge, was seated there.

By 1976, McFetridge was long dead. Because of tightened security, his methods would have been too primitive to have worked at Madison Square Garden. Not only had it become difficult to get on the Convention floor, or even into the Convention building, but the ancient practice of having a courier fill his pockets with the credentials of delegates and alternates, going off the floor to distribute these to favored persons who needed them to get in, was no longer the open sesame it once was; the Convention floor was now so heavily laced with security people, a valid delegate who had lent his credentials could be easily spotted and quickly expelled.

In any case, Daley was lacking the Convention seats in 1976 that he felt he was entitled to have received. A small affront, perhaps, on the part of the National Committee, but irritating to Daley nonetheless—Daley interpreting this as a deliberate effort on the part of Strauss or the Carter forces to humiliate him, as Paul Butler had tried to do in Los Angeles in 1960. "That's no way to treat us," Daley complained to state chairman Touhy, although there was nothing that Touhy could do to provide Daley with his precious tickets. Young William Daley, acting on orders from his father, conferred with Michael J. Howlett, Jr., in hope that through his contacts, which were different from Daley's—through his closer relationship to the Jimmy Carter people, perhaps—Howlett Senior might have a source. Young Howlett said no, they had no tickets. Receiving this news from his son, Daley nodded grimly and went downstairs to have dinner with his family in the Bull and Bear of the Waldorf.

Next morning, Monday, July 12, Daley got a phone call from Mike Howlett, who said, "I think I'm getting ten tickets to the Convention. They're planning to change the tickets for every session, so we'll have to play it day by day; but I've been promised that we'll be taken care of." Daley was delighted. Howlett's source was a Washington, D.C., newsman who had a connection to the people in charge of credentials. That afternoon, Howlett got a phone call from the lobby; his source said, "I've got the merchandise." Young Mike was dispatched to pick up the tickets.

That afternoon, and every afternoon of Convention week, a transfer was worked out at a meeting in the Howlett suite between young Michael Howlett and young William Daley. Arriving at the garage level of the Waldorf on the first night of the Convention, Howlett was greeted by a hearty smile from Daley, who was waiting for his limousine to draw up. "Good work on the tickets, Mike," Daley said, chortling.

"It's great to be back," Richard Daley declared, as floor reporters crowded around his chair under the standard of the Illinois delegation. "It is like I have never been away and we are going to have a great Convention and a great candidate for president." From all areas of the floor, delegates made their way through the crowded aisles to Daley's side. The broadcasting network floor people, tiny, strange-world antennae sticking up over their headsets, converged on the leader of the Illinois Democrats.

The Reverend Jesse Jackson, a principal in the 1972 revolt to exclude the Daley 59 from the Convention in Miami Beach, made a ceremony of shaking hands with Daley. Governor Walker, who had scorned Daley as few other men ever did, wore a fawning smile as he gushed that it was good to see the Mayor in his old place of honor. Chicago reporters gazed disbelieving as old enemies bestowed upon Daley a kiss of peace; it was a little much—this show of affection by Jackson and Walker. Yet— "We are all members of the Democratic party," the Mayor had responded. "We are all workin' for the same things," he declared. "As you can see for yourself," he went on, "we got a united party." A Chicago reporter demurred; it looked to him, he said, as if the deep wounds that the Illinois Democrats had inflicted on each other were being covered up with Band-Aids. Daley shook his head. "Not any of your Band-Aids," he replied. "You will see, when the campaign develops, we are held together by steel."

At the Democrats' mini-convention in Kansas City in December 1974, Daley had been regarded as a vital caisson in the effort to rebuild the party structure that had been so badly damaged by the McGovern temblor of 1972. There was anxious deference paid to Daley in Kansas City, as party leaders waited for a sign from this man who had been so badly treated at Miami Beach that he was willing to forgive and be conciliatory. There had been nothing artificial about the applause greeting Daley's speech which said that bygones must be bygones; that there was room for dissent within the Democratic party; that dedicated people, working together, could go forward to victory.

Hardly anyone at Kansas City had ever heard of Jimmy Carter. Those who had would have dismissed as nonsense the possibility that the one-term governor of Georgia would emerge, eighteen months later, as the man on whom their hopes of regaining control of the national government would depend. In December 1974, Daley had been a mountain and Carter was a mouse. By July 1976, Carter was the mountain and Daley was a museum piece.

At the Democratic Convention in New York in July of 1976,

even children had the temerity to confront the once-unapproachable Daley. Two twelve-year-olds, a girl named Lee Heh Margolies and a boy named John Engle, braced him for an interview on the Convention floor. The kids had media credentials, and cardboard floor passes were hanging from strings around their necks, the same as adult reporters who had access to the floor. Daley was mystified when they moved in, asking if they could interview him for the *Children's Express.* Daley's sons, rising from the seats they had taken directly behind him, peered with suspicion as he cheerfully consented to be interviewed. Ever wary of ingenious attempts to entrap the old man, the Daley boys appeared not quite comfortable with the idea of the Mayor's setting himself up for interrogation by two pre-puberty reporters. Somehow, the thing didn't ring true; two kids interviewing the Mayor? *Kids?* Next day, with publication of a Democratic Convention "special" of the *Children's Express,* the Daley boys had reason to regret that they hadn't risked the ire of the old man by making an effort to abort this interview.

DALEY ON '68:
'IT NEVER HAPPENED'

This was the block-type front-page headline of the juvenile journal, with a verbatim report of the questions put to Daley by Lee Heh Margolies and his self-serving replies:

LEE HEH MARGOLIES: How many conventions have you been to?

MAYOR RICHARD DALEY: A number of them dear . . . starting back in 1928.

LHM: Which one do you think was the most interesting for you?

DALEY: Well, they're all interesting—but the one in 1948 and the one in 1960 and then one in 1932. The election of Franklin Delano Roosevelt.

LHM: I heard about the convention in 1968 in Chicago and there was something . . .

DALEY: Don't believe everything you hear dear . . . Ha Ha Ha.

LHM: I know but there was supposed to have been—Well the majority of people I've interviewed—There were supposed to have been lots of riots and demonstrations.

DALEY: Well, that isn't true.

LHM: Why isn't that true?

DALEY: The media and the newspapers are the ones who...
LHM: Well, it's other people than the media.
DALEY: Well, they were the ones that depict the story. They were the ones who described the rioting.
LHM: Well, could you describe to me what it was like?
DALEY: Well, we're in a different age in history, a different era today. This is 1976; that's eight years ago, so we like to talk about what the future of our country is and not go back and talk about the problems in '68. We've got so many things to do today, it's more important than talking about ancient history.
LHM: Who would you want to be president?
DALEY: James Carter—Jimmy Carter.
LHM: Who do you think will win the Republican nomination?
DALEY: I don't know; that's up to the Republicans.
LHM: I know, but Democrats have opinions, too.
DALEY: Yes, they do. But I have no opinion. (End interview.)

CHICAGO MAYOR
CLOSES EYES,
REWRITES
HISTORY

In a sidebar to the Margolies interrogation of Daley, the *Children's Express* presented the impressions of twelve-year-old reporter John Engle, who stood at Ms. Margolies' side:

I think that one of the reasons that kids get interviews is because the people they're interviewing don't expect them to ask questions that are bad for them. I don't think Mayor Daley expected Lee Heh to ask him about why he didn't do something about the riots in '68. She asked him about the riots and I could see his face—it changed. At first, he apparently thought that Lee Heh was going to ask him how old he was and do you like your job. I could see his face—he was really startled when she asked him about the riots in '68. He was very uncomfortable and he started looking the other way. I don't think he thought Lee Heh could have asked that question. He thought she was too young to know about all that. I know he denied that there were any riots in '68. That's absolutely untrue. But I think he said he didn't want to be asked any more questions after that.

In many ways, the opening day of the Convention had been tedious for Richard J. Daley. He had hardly had breakfast before a message came in from his office in Chicago that John Cardinal Cody, Daley's ecclesiastical counterpart, was attempting to exorcise the devil of abortion from the Democratic party platform and was more or less attempting to brand Jimmy Carter as a right-to-life infidel. The poached eggs, Daley's customary breakfast, churned in Daley's stomach as he heard that His Eminence was bent on hurting Carter's chances of getting a heavy vote from Chicago Catholics in November.

The *Chicago Daily News* had a report on the front page that Cody had snubbed Daley by rejecting his invitation to give the invocation at Mike Howlett's fund-raising dinner on July 1. The Cardinal had spurned Daley's invitation, the newspaper said, when he learned that Carter, gravely at odds with the Catholic hierarchy on the gut issue of abortion, had curtly sent word through an administrative assistant that he would not appear with Carter.

The fact is that it was Howlett who had received the turndown, the *Daily News* being in error on this, because it had been at Howlett's invitation, not Daley's, that Cody was invited to the dinner. Now, two weeks later, Howlett was receiving telephone calls in New York from his assistant secretary of state, Martin J. McLaughlin, in Chicago. McLaughlin, in communication with Cody's office, had been told that Cody was highly displeased at Daley's apparent endorsement of Jimmy Carter's refusal to support a constitutional amendment to nullify the United States Supreme Court opinion that abortion is a woman's right, available on demand. So far as Cardinal Cody was concerned, Daley was surrendering religious principle to political expediency. Cody apparently had decided that Daley, in his scramble to gain a favorable place alongside an ex-Georgia governor who seemed on his way to the presidency, was willing to subjugate his devotion to Mother Church, rather than jeopardize his chances of gaining a place with Carter in the sanctuary of politics.

Howlett telephoned Daley's suite to advise the Mayor that the Cardinal, so much like Daley in his exercise of authority, was freely discussing his displeasure with the Chicago Democrats and that this posed a threat, in Howlett's opinion, to the traditionally large Democratic vote that would be needed in November. Howlett discovered Daley to be remarkably unconcerned. "It's nuthin', Mike," the Mayor had reassured Howlett. "It'll all blow over."

Howlett had expected that Daley would be concerned and he had expected to discuss with Daley the Cody problem, passing on to him confidential information that McLaughlin had gleaned from Cody's office. It did not strike Howlett that abortion was a problem that could be expected to vanish; as a candidate for governor, Howlett was seriously concerned. However, in view of Daley's indifference, he thought it useless to pursue the matter and held his tongue.

The disturbing information that McLaughlin had received was that Cody and Terence Cardinal Cooke of New York were in constant communication on the matter of how to get the abortion plank onto the floor of the Convention, where such prominent delegates as Richard Daley would be forced to take a position. McLaughlin had learned that Jimmy Carter had dispatched the Reverend Andrew Young, the black congressman who was his confidant, to confer with Cooke, to plead the argument that he, Carter, was personally against abortion. The New York Cardinal, McLaughlin had been told, had been gracious to Young, but privately annoyed that Carter had sent a black emissary and had not come to argue his own case. Even so, it did not appear that Carter was indifferent, as Daley was, toward an issue that could hurt the Democratic party in the election, in November.

McLaughlin had learned, from a source in Cody's office— information being leaked deliberately to McLaughlin for transmission to Daley and Howlett in New York—that word was speeding through the sacred grapevine of the Catholic hierarchy that Roman Catholic clergy would be expected to decline invitations to be present at any political function at which any pro-abortion candidate of either party was to be the principal speaker.

McLaughlin had mentioned, in talking to his boss, Howlett, that a Reverend Robert N. Deming of the Church of the Immaculate Conception in Kansas City, Missouri, was on the Convention's Wednesday night agenda—to deliver the benediction that would close the session at which Jimmy Carter would be nominated. McLaughlin said it was his information that this Father Deming wouldn't show—and, in passing, it can be noted that Deming did not show and that no other Catholic clergyman had shown up to invoke God's blessing on the Democratic Convention, a snub that the most senior delegates could not recall ever having happened at a presidential nominating convention.

Daley hardly glanced, during the hours before the convening of the first session at Madison Square Garden, at the abortion plank in the Democratic party platform. Throughout the day, the right-to-life proponents, holed up in their tiny headquarters in the Statler-Hilton, tried in vain to reach Daley by phone to plead with him to support their cause on the Convention floor. In a sullen silence, Daley remained secluded in his suite at the Waldorf. He was now aware that Cardinal Cody was striving to put pressure on him, back in Chicago, his City Hall office having advised him of the effort the intractable Cardinal was making to rebuke Carter. Howlett confided to his own people that Daley had not made much of a response to the report he had received on what Cody was up to, but Howlett suspected that Daley was "mad as a sonofabitch at Cody, for butting into politics."

Hy Raskin had grinned, at hearing Howlett's report on this. "Daley's losing his cool," Raskin said. "He hasn't got much of a hold on Carter and Cody is fucking it up." Howlett laughed and said, "What Cody doesn't understand is that out in Daley's ward, you got to be loyal to God and Country and the Democratic Party—but not necessarily in that order."

Down in the Waldorf lobby, Daley's Chicago delegates were passing the time in idle conversation, oblivious to the moral-political dilemma that confronted their self-isolated leader. Occasionally, one would say, "What do you hear?" And someone would reply, "Nuthin'." To which the first one would say, "Me, too; nuthin'." Placid and bored, they had heard vague stories that there seemed to be trouble of some kind about the question of abortion, but this was not the kind of issue that excited any of them. Abortion? What would that matter to someone like tough-looking John d'Arco, Democratic committeeman of Chicago's First Ward, holding power of sorts, as the crime syndicate's man, over the downtown area of the city? He was satisfied to create an impression that he knew what was going on, which he did, a cynical smile on his face, as Howlett, Raskin, and Touhy stepped out of an elevator, d'Arco asking, "How is it going, Mike?" Howlett had smiled and said, "Everything is fine, John; everything is working out real good." Outwardly, this appeared to be true.

Over lunch in the Bull and Bear, Howlett, Touhy, and Raskin traded stories of various Chicago politicians of the old days, all of them laughing at Touhy's account of a Jewish bookmaker who had fled to the South to avoid getting murdered by syndicate gangsters and who had become highly influential by enlisting, under a non-Jewish name, in the Ku Klux Klan—"playing the percentages all the way." The lighthearted conversation was threaded, however, with references to Daley's struggle to escape embarrassment on the abortion issue. "You would think," Howlett observed, "that Daley would recognize that what we are doing here at this Convention is denying a minority group the right to be heard. What kind of a Convention have we got, when Democrats have no chance to be heard?"

Hy Raskin put a match to his cigar and was pensive as he said, "The Carter people are afraid that if they bend on the abortion thing, they'll have to bend on letting the fags get up there on the platform to talk about their thing. Carter is too smart to let this thing turn into a circus for the queers, for Christ's sake." Jack Touhy agreed. "Well," he said, "the Carter people have locked everybody out through the rules; they took care to shut out Pro Life and The Queers in drawing up the rules. But they've got Daley in the middle, with Cody chewing his ass out back in Chicago. "Look," Raskin replied, "there is only one way for Daley to go: he's got to stay with the Carter people or he ends up with nothing when Carter is elected. In politics, it is not what power you used to have; the only thing that counts is what power you've got right now. Daley had his shot at doing something for Carter during the primaries, when Carter needed him. Now Carter doesn't need him; Christ Almighty, he won't even need Daley in November; he will win, even if he fails to carry Illinois. Daley can't take the chance of going against Carter on this abortion; for once in his life, Daley is screwed, either way he goes."

At Madison Square Garden that evening, two delegates from Missouri crossed the aisle to the Illinois delegation and spoke to Howlett. Missouri was circulating a petition, calling on the Convention to permit a minority report on the hands-off abortion plank that Carter's people had worked into the party platform. Howlett read the petition, took out a pen, and signed it. He handed the petition to Lieutenant Governor Neil Hartigan, who read it, hesitated, and then with a frown of resignation signed it. Cecil Partee, president of the Illinois Senate and Daley's candidate for attorney general, took the petition from Howlett and signed it. Jack Touhy added his signature. Howlett then leaned over toward Daley and said, "I think you might want to sign this; it won't do any good, but I think we should sign this." "On the abortion?" asked Daley. Howlett nodded. "They won't allow any discussion on the abortion," Daley said. Howlett agreed. Daley signed it and Howlett passed the petition to Illinois delegates in the back rows, some signing and some passing it on with not so much as a glance at what it said.

Howlett was aware that Daley was in a dark mood. Daley appeared to be impassive; inwardly, he had reason for despair. Compounding his fears that Cardinal Cody's persistence on the abortion question might sever the tenuous connection that Daley was striving to maintain with the obdurate Jimmy Carter, Daley was brooding over depressing news from Chicago that federal Judge William J. Lynch, his boyhood chum and former law partner, was in critical condition in the intensive-care unit of St. Joseph's Hospital. Federal Appeals Court Judge William J. Bauer, investigating Lynch's unexplained absence from his court,

had discovered Lynch in a state of unconsciousness on the bed-
room floor of his bachelor apartment on North Lake Shore
Drive. Shaved, wearing shorts, Lynch apparently had been
dressing when, somehow, he had taken a bad fall. There was a
massive contusion on Lynch's head and it was instantly apparent
to Bauer that his friend Lynch was in serious condition.

Word that Lynch was in bad shape had come from Dr. Eric
Oldberg. "The sister superior at St. Joseph's had called me,"
Oldberg disclosed, in recalling, months later, his part in this affair. "I had been Dick's source of information on Lynch the first
time they had him in St. Joseph's for this thing; the sister up
there would call me and I would call Dick. So, when it happened again, with Dick attending his Convention in New York,
she called me again.

"It was the same old thing; he had been drinking, of course,
and he had another sub-dural hematoma, which is a characteristic of drinkers—they fall and hit their heads and bleeding starts,
producing a clot that acts like a rapidly growing brain tumor.
All you can do is put a hole in the fellow's head and you have
to be quick about it; that's what was done for Lynch when he
had his fall a couple of years earlier. This time, during the Convention, he was worse off than before and you could tell that he
would never come out of it—at least as a functioning human
being. But the sister would call me every morning at 6:45 and I
would relay the message to Daley in New York.

Dr. Oldberg said that he didn't talk to Daley on his calls to
New York; he gave the message to the Mayor's daughter Mary
Carol, who was married to a doctor and who was in New York
with the family for the Convention. The sum of his morning
reports was that if Judge Lynch survived, it was highly likely
that he would be a vegetable. Daley—he thought—had now
given up on Lynch.

"Lynch had been exceedingly close to the Daleys; his father
and Dick's father used to go fishing together, and the boys had
been lifelong pals. At all the fancy dinners and things, there
would be Lynch at the table with the family. When Lynch had
been in the hospital the first time, Daley had gone up to the
hospital every day to visit with him and that was an heroic kind

of thing for a busy man to do. But this second time, while Dick was in New York for the Convention— Well, I guess the Daleys just gave up on Lynch as a lost cause; they recognized now that he was an alcoholic and, like Matt Danaher, you know, who had given them the same problem, I think you could say that the Daleys decided Lynch had just outlived his usefulness."

Sitting with Daley on the Convention floor, aware of Lynch's condition, Mike Howlett and Jack Touhy were mystified by the casual manner in which Daley discussed the matter. Daley spoke about Lynch as if he were a stranger, showing no emotion as he relayed the Oldberg diagnosis that, even if he came out of it, Lynch was doomed to be a vegetable. "Daley didn't act as if he gave a damn about Lynch and it was hard to understand why he wasn't upset about it," Howlett said. "He was a real cold potato about it. Here he was, with his best friend in bad shape and Daley having no feeling about it.

"It was like the way Daley was in politics. You never knew where the hell Daley was going when he pushed somebody into a political battle. You never knew whether he wanted his man to win or whether he was setting him up to be beaten, by way of getting rid of him. I couldn't believe that he didn't care what happened to Lynch, but he seemed to have no feeling about it."

Daley was still capable, however, of displaying other emotions. He made it clear to Howlett, midway in Convention week, that he was highly annoyed with him. Howlett had been interviewed at length on television, reaffirming his anti-Carter position on abortion. Asked if he had backed off his opposition to abortion, Howlett had replied that, no, he had not. Asked if he thought there was a possibility of serious trouble at the Convention on the abortion issue, Howlett said, well, there was a great deal of anti-platform talk in many of the delegations. Did Howlett think the right-to-life people were justified in seeking a chance to state their case to the Convention? Yes, he did; it was a practice of the Democratic party, he said, to allow minority groups to present their views—this tolerance was what the Democratic party was all about. Did Howlett think that Carter was worried about having abortion develop into a serious election issue? Well, if Carter wasn't worried, he should be, Howlett had replied; his position might cost him a lot of votes in Illinois.

Would Howlett expect Mayor Daley to stand up and be counted in opposition to Carter's stand on abortion, if it came to that? Howlett said he didn't know what Daley would do; every man has to speak for himself—"I don't tell Daley any orders and Mayor Daley doesn't give Mike Howlett any orders, on abortion or anything else." Daley had been displeased to hear from Chicago that the Howlett interview had been carried by a TV station there, in full, the word from Chicago being that Howlett's remarks had made Daley look bad.

Daley was aggravated that Howlett would continue to flaunt his independence of Daley; couldn't a man be grateful to someone who had engineered his nomination to run for governor? And other aggravations were filling the famous big-city boss with doubts of his invincibility.

He had spent a lifetime measuring the fading influence of once-powerful Democratic politicians and he was not so insensitive to the signs of change that he did not detect, in brief conversations with members of the Old Guard who came over from other delegations to shake his hand, that he was regarded by them as merely another member of the alumni of yesteryear big shots who had been eased out of the Democratic party's inner circle.

Looking over his shoulder at the Young Turks of his own organization, clustered along the wall at the rear of the Illinois delegation space—watching them take turns posturing as he postured, knowing from his grapevine that they were mimicking his bumbling, ungrammatical speech, some of them so good at this that they sounded more like Daley than Daley—he would have preferred that they take their seats and try to be attentive to Convention business, as he was trying to do.

Daley was annoyed that his caustic critic, lame duck Governor Dan Walker, was delegation-hopping all over the floor and that Walker was attempting to ingratiate himself with Carter, having made impassioned speeches to *twenty-three* state caucuses, urging these Convention delegates to do their utmost for Jimmy's election after he was nominated. "My God," Daley complained to Jack Touhy, "what's he think he's doing? Where's the loyalty?

Where's the good of the party? Don't he remember what happened, in the primary, with Howlett as our candidate for the governor—and Walker not even a delegate?"

Daley was angry that Chicago media people had got hold of a story that he was trying in a confidential way to negotiate peace with yet another enemy, Congressman Ralph Metcalfe of Chicago's mostly black South Side. For four years, Metcalfe, who had once been a loyal organization man, had been blistering Daley with accusations that he was permitting, if not promoting, police brutality in the ghettos. Daley had tried and failed to knock Metcalfe out of office—as recently as the March 16 primary. Now, it was accurately being reported, Daley was attempting to negotiate a truce—having told the black Congressman during the Illinois delegation reception at the Waldorf on Sunday: "Ralph, we'll be sitting down soon." The leak on what Daley had said to Metcalfe could only have come from Metcalfe and Daley was furious, his personal conviction confirmed that you could not trust any of the "coloreds" to keep a confidence.

Daley was annoyed, finally, that Senator Adlai E. Stevenson III was holding himself aloof from the Convention. What was the matter with Stevenson, he asked Howlett, that he refused to come and take his seat like everyone else? Actually, Stevenson had come to Madison Square Garden on opening night of the Convention. He had stood in the aisle and surveyed the Illinois delegation. Discovering that someone else was in his seat near Daley and that there was no other vacant seat available, he had shrugged and gone back to the hotel, not to be seen again until the closing night, when political protocol required that he make an appearance.

As Stevenson, holed up at the Waldorf, looked at the Convention on television only when he felt like it, Daley was in his chair at the Garden in advance of opening gavel at every session. Even if he didn't like what was going on, he feigned interest. Daley sat as if hypnotized, for example, as the black Congresswoman Barbara Jordan (D., Texas), her diction slicing through the hubbub like a switchblade knife, electrified the Convention with a brilliant keynote speech, the delegates flooding her with applause that was not to be equaled at any time during the Convention. Expression never changing, Daley pounded his palms together, along with everyone else. When it was over, the keynoter grinning in triumph as she waved a black hand, Jack Touhy swung his head toward Daley and said, "Great speech." Daley did not reply.

Hours later, back at the Waldorf, Touhy asked Mary Mullen if she had heard Barbara Jordan and she nodded, noncommittally. "Great speech," Touhy remarked. Snapping back like a Bridgeport whip, Ms. Mullen sneered, "I guess it was all right— if you like niggers." Revealing this brief exchange at a luncheon table next day, Touhy said, "Even Daley seems to know that the old days are gone, but I think Mary is going to be the last one to surrender."

For his part, Richard Daley had reason to suspect that Senator Stevenson might be the last one to surrender. This had been the day, opening day of the Convention, that Stevenson had paid his prescribed visit to the Americana Hotel suite of candidate Carter. Returning to the Waldorf, the Senator had gone directly to his rooms and, sending an aide to fetch bagels and corned beef from a deli, had thereafter remained in seclusion. Adlai had confided to his wife, Nancy, that the discussion with Carter was pretty much a rehash of their conversation in the dining room of the Stevenson home in Washington, back in May. "He continues to intrigue me with the question of what kind of president *I* would be, if something happened to him and I had to succeed him." In a terse phone call to Daley, Stevenson limited himself to saying that he had had a short visit with Carter, it had been pleasant, and now he was back. Eager for information and getting none from the taciturn Stevenson, Daley huskily declared, "Well, I'm still pulling for you." Hanging up, Adlai gave a wry glance to Nancy and said, emotionlessly, "Daley is pulling for me." Nancy laughed.

Tuesday of Convention week began for Daley on a slightly better note; Howlett had called to say that he would be having breakfast next morning with Governor Walker at Walker's hotel, the Warwick. Tuesday night, Daley was to have a moment of glory, being one of the two speakers who were scheduled to address the delegates on the desperate plight of the major cities.

He was to speak to the frightening and rising incidence of unemployment among blacks and Spanish in the urban centers, the urgent need for federal funding of mass transit systems, the unbearable financial burden of maintaining public schools, the losing battle that the big cities were waging to provide adequate housing for low-income people— It was a rather good speech somebody had written for him, but Daley was noticeably edgy about his chances of making a good impression on the national television audience. He had rehearsed the speech and was hopeful that he would read it well, but this would be the first time since his angry put-down of Walter Cronkite of CBS, at the riotous 1968 Convention in Chicago, that the nation would get a good look at him. In Bridgeport terms, this was Daley's chance to get even and show himself off as a man who knew as much as any man could know of the nation's critical urban crises. This was Daley's big chance, and he was visibly nervous as he got up from his chair and headed, with escort, toward the podium.

In a futile try at exhibiting themselves as the raucous, devil-may-care Chicago Democrats of old, Daley's people began whooping things up as their leader disappeared from view. "We're gonna give this Convention an old-fashioned demonstration, to let 'em see how Daley stands with us," one of the Chicago ward bosses declared. Magically, placards appeared among the delegates:

Daley for President!

MR. DEMOCRAT—DALEY

We Love Our Boss!

HIZZONER FOREVER!

Daley—20 More Years!

These makeshift signs, held over the heads of the delegates who had crudely inscribed the lettering, drew a cold stare from Daley's sons, who seemed to sense that this display was juvenile, if not a mockery of their father. The elder generation of the Chicago Democrats—Howlett, Touhy, Marzullo, d'Arco—

ignored the pathetic attempt at high jinks that was going on in the seats behind them; it was as if the older Democrats, accustomed to their professional methods, regarded these antics as an act of self-ridicule, an evil omen that even his own people regarded Daley as a disintegrating political boss who could safely be humiliated.

Many of the media people on the Convention floor—still photographers, television reporters, and the like—worked their way through the aisles to see what the commotion in the Illinois delegation was all about, then sized up the situation and turned away. What did it matter that the Chicago Democrats were making fools of themselves, as their famous leader stood before the Convention making a speech?

"Great speech," Mike Howlett complimented Daley, when he returned from the podium. "Great speech," said Jack Touhy. "Fine speech, Mr. Mayor," said Alderman Michael Bilandic, of Daley's 11th Ward—the man chosen by Daley to be leader of Chicago's City Council when Tom Keane had been led off to federal prison. "Fine, fine," Daley responded. "T'anks, t'anks." And, satisfied that he had done well, he folded his arms and turned his attention to the Convention platform.

At the rear of the Illinois delegation space, the Young Turks who had wandered across the street from Madison Square Garden for drinks, were wandering back in again, taking up standing room along the wall, which they had discovered to be a more comfortable way of enduring the session than getting locked into a seat. The Young Turks asked when Daley was going to speak to the Convention. "He done it already," someone said; "didn't you see it on the television?" Exchanging glances, the Young Turks shook their heads. "They didn't put him on television," one of the Young Turks said. "They didn't think he was important enough for television."

The band played "Happy Days Are Here Again!" as the Democratic Convention geared up Wednesday night to nominate Jimmy Carter, Daley in his seat at Madison Square Garden before the opening gavel of the session sounded. Daley, looking tired, sat with arms folded in the posture of a deposed king who was stunned by the discovery that his happy days were slipping away.

He was pleased to have had a brief meeting with Jacqueline Kennedy Onassis, who had appeared genuinely courteous to Daley. This had been good for his ego, awakening thoughts of the triumphal days when Jack was president. Senator Edward Kennedy of Massachusetts also revived Daley's thoughts of what used to be, by paying him a visit on the Convention floor. Yet, the appearance of Senator Kennedy, unattended by Secret Service escort, was yet another sign that the old order had changed; Teddy Kennedy didn't carry much weight now, either. Daley's last grip on political importance, nationally, now appeared to depend upon grasping the possible vice-presidential coattails of Adlai Stevenson, and Stevenson was indifferent to the matter of whether or not Daley succeeded in hanging on.

Despite the accommodation that Daley had reached with young Stevenson years earlier, when Republican Senator Everett McKinley Dirksen had died and Daley decided that the regular Democrats had no better option than to support the frigid and sometimes caustic Young Adlai for Dirksen's place, Daley had continued to be annoyed at young Stevenson's unchanging attitude of indifference toward him. Now, with evening shadows falling on Daley's career, the aging boss was dependent for a Washington connection upon a young patrician who seemed to regard him with disdain.

In the Richard J. Daley scheme of politics, all others were expendable. Now, it appeared, *he* was expendable. His reflex had always been to make the best possible readjustment when death, tragedy, or other circumstances removed those upon whom he had depended. Whatever sorrow he might have had at the demise of a lengthy list of superiors and cronies—some of whom had contributed greatly to his political advancement, some of whom had died when they were impeding it—Daley seemingly had been born with some kind of gyroscope that quickly put him back on course. There had been speculation, when President Kennedy was assassinated in 1963, for example, that Daley would go into prolonged shock over the loss of a president that he had proudly claimed as his personal friend. However grievous a blow Kennedy's death had been to Daley, he had managed a quick reconciliation with the new president, Lyndon B. Johnson, and, while this new relationship was devoid of sentimentality, there was no slippage in the gears of the Daley machine. Daley's rule was that he would always do what was best for Daley.

Dealing with the grim business of divorcing himself from one of his early patrons, Adlai E. Stevenson II—refusing to make the ex-Governor's dethronement more graceful and dignified, as a considerate man would have felt obligated to do; refusing to go through the motions at the Los Angeles Convention in 1960 of offering his erstwhile benefactor even token support for the presidency, fearful of losing his gamble that John F. Kennedy would win the nomination—a stony-faced Richard Daley had not trifled with any need for charity.

Confronted now, sixteen years later, with the disquieting business of ingratiating himself with the Governor's *son*—having had evidence during the past decade that Adlai III was less conciliatory, in every way tougher, than Adlai II had been—Daley was frustrated at the 1976 Convention as he waited for Carter to name his man for vice-president, the young Senator Stevenson acting as if he had not the slightest interest in being Carter's choice. Daley had been weaned on the strong political milk that when there is an office that you want, you fight and scratch and bring in your friends to help you get it; how could a man who might be vice-president—God knows what this might lead to: the presidency, in due course, perhaps—be so casual about this that he would not even discuss the possibilities, would not let Daley even taste the cookie of anticipation?

In the course of the presidential nominating speeches and seconding speeches on Wednesday night of the Convention, Mike Howlett nudged Daley with an elbow and, gesturing with the back of his head to the Madison Square Garden gallery, he said, "Walker's up there with the alternates, waiting to lead the cheers when Carter gets it." Daley had grunted, as if to say that he did not wish to think about Dan Walker. Howlett had given Daley a briefing on his breakfast meeting that morning with Walker, Daley nodding when he heard that Walker had said he planned to campaign for Howlett, but not *with* Howlett; Walker saying that he would be working one part of the state, while Mike was electioneering somewhere else—adding that he would have to work out his schedule on the basis of what free time would be available, Walker implying that his obligation to campaign for Carter would have priority. "It isn't much that he is promising us, but at least it gets him off my back." Daley nodded again and said, "Dat's good, dat's good."

Walker leaped to his feet, his wife alongside him, and applauded with great energy when the roll call reached the point where Carter won nomination—Ohio supplying 132 of its 152 votes to push Carter past the 1,505 votes that were needed. If Daley had sad remembrances that he had held off until after Carter's victory in the Ohio primary before throwing his support to Carter; if Daley had regrets that he had failed to recognize Carter's potential at an earlier date, when he might have placed Carter in his political debt, Daley did not mention this. An expressionless Daley applauded the vote of Ohio that put Jimmy Carter over the top; almost certainly, the Democrats had a nominee who would be elected president, but Daley had done nothing for him and had no claim on him. Reporting the Convention vote for Illinois, sixteenth of the delegations to be called, and the first of the big states to be overwhelmingly for Carter, chairman Daley had announced 164 of the 169 Illinois votes for Carter, as the Convention cheered. But Carter was to finish in the roll call with 2,200 votes, 700 more than were needed for nomination, and it did not matter what kind of count Illinois gave him. Methodically clapping his hands, Mike Howlett turned to Jack Touhy as the band played "Happy Days Are Here Again!" and said, "In a pig's fat ass, happy days are here again."

Adlai Stevenson said he was sitting on the edge of a bed, munching a sweet roll, when the call from Jimmy Carter came about 8:45 A.M. Thursday. "He was gracious and said he was sorry to tell me that he had chosen someone else." Had Senator Stevenson asked Carter who the choice for vice-president would be? "No, certainly not." Was the Senator disappointed? "Yes, I suppose you could say that I was disappointed. But I was also relieved; my kids are relieved. I had an ambivalence regarding all of this; I have a certain independence as a senator that I would not have had as vice-president. I didn't lose any sleep—

until, perhaps, last night, when I got very curious and impatient to get it over with." Had he called Mayor Daley? "Not right away. I told Nancy, my wife, and let the kids know that I had not been chosen. I finished my sweet roll and had some coffee then, and I finished dressing; I had been walking around in my pants and a pair of socks. Then I think it was that I called Daley." Was Daley disappointed? "Well, I suppose he was; they say he was rather eager to have me slated for vice-president. All I can remember that he said to me was that he had been 'hopin' I would be the one." Pressed as to whether Daley had been counting on him to be his Washington connection, Adlai III smiled.

Daley accepted with equanimity Carter's choice of Senator Walter Mondale for vice-president. "Mondale is as strong as Stevenson," he told reporters, hastily adding, "but we love Stevenson, of course." There had been persistent reports that Daley had tried to convince Carter that he would be assured of victory in Illinois if he had Stevenson as his running mate. Stevenson had joked about being regarded as "Daley's pet rock."

Not even the Chicago reporters had any interest in talking to the great Richard J. Daley as he sat under the Illinois standard Thursday night of the Convention, as Mondale was nominated and then spoke, nominee Carter following him to the podium. This was only the second Democratic Convention that Carter had attended and the old pros, like Daley, were confounded by the manner in which he had maneuvered them out of power. "It is a time for healing," Carter intoned, but not necessarily for the mortal wounds that he and his crowd had inflicted upon the Old Guard.

The final night must have seemed endless to Richard Daley—although this likely would be the last time that Daley would attend a presidential nominating convention; the same as Jake Arvey and all of the others who had fallen out of prominence, the seventy-four-year-old Daley was through. Oh, he would make a show of embracing Jimmy Carter on his campaign visits to Chicago; there would be the traditional parade for his Democratic candidate and all of that. But, looking at Boss Daley, as he allowed his eyes to take in one last view of the Convention floor, an observer would have thought Daley was weary and old and discouraged. Nationally, he was finished.

Next morning, on the 26th floor of the Waldorf, there was an accidental meeting of Daley and Howlett. Freshly shaved, sharply dressed, Daley greeted Howlett with a cheery, "Hi ya, Mike," and a quick shake of the hands. He declared without conviction: "Great Convention. We got a fine candidate. He's gonna help us, Carter, a great candidate from the South workin' with us and needin' us—"

Howlett gently responded, "Yeah, that's right."

Then, with emphasis, Daley announced, "I'm gettin' out; I'm going home. So it's over, and what is there for somebody to do? Go home."

Howlett nodded. "Yeah, you're right. And that's just what I'm going to do."

"Johnny Touhy's at the meetin', the Carter meetin'. He'll go and let us know—the campaign plans and all of that. It was a great Convention, so I'm going home."

And he and Howlett shook hands and parted.

Chapter Five

"It's the kiss of death to have a Daley connection. You can't fight with him, or you're liable to lose Chicago. If you don't get his arm off your back, you're a cinch to lose outside of Chicago."

—Michael J. Howlett

THE CHICAGO DEMOCRATS returned to their home city from the New York Convention with a sense of foreboding. They had been accustomed to Daley's maneuvering at the highest levels of their political world, and now it was apparent that Daley's strength had been sapped by the Jimmy Carter victory. Moreover, Daley was acting queerly.

To more than one, Daley boasted that it was he who had decided when he would undergo surgery as he lay in critical condition in Rush-Presbyterian-St. Luke's Hospital in mid-1974. A small thing, perhaps, but they felt it strange that this secretive boss would confide in them now that it was he who set the day and the hour for his endarterectomy, recounting the details of how the operation had been arranged as if it had occurred yesterday, rather than two years previously.

Why, they wondered, would he now reveal that he had had suspicions that someone might be plotting to destroy him as he lay helpless on the operating table? For what purpose did Daley think that members of his organization should be told, two years after the operation, that he had cleverly outwitted his unnamed enemies?

"They didn't know, the doctors, what somebody might be planning," Daley had said, telling his story to two of the Democratic Young Turks who rode with him one summer day in 1976 to a funeral. "They think all it is was bringing a fellow in, putting him under the ether, and doing it. All they are thinking about is their part, getting it over with; they aren't thinking about somebody wanting to hurt you and how they would do it, with you laying there helpless and not able to fight them off. What do the doctors know? Only what they have to do, if they do it right; that's all they know."

Listening to this recital, the Young Turks had been goggle-eyed. Later, discovering that Daley had confided to Jack Touhy and others the same bizarre tale of outfoxing his unseen enemies, the Young Turks took to exchanging wry jokes that "Oscar"—as the Young Turks privately referred to Daley—had become paranoid. "He always had this thing about not trusting anyone," Alderman Edward Vrdolyak observed, "but now it looks like the old man is losing his marbles."

Even if he believed, as apparently he did, that in some mysterious way he would be assassinated, and that he had had to conceive a strategy to thwart this evil plot, the Daley they knew would normally have told them nothing. Yet, riding along in his limousine in a funeral procession, he had talked openly about a secret so personal he once would have hesitated to mention it to even Mrs. Daley.

"I ask them when is the time when nothing is happening at the hospital and the doctors say it is on Sunday. I ask them, 'What time on Sunday?' and they say in the morning, or in the afternoon. I ask them what happens if they've got me there, in the operatin', and all of a sudden the power goes out? They don't know what I'm thinking, but *I* know. All right; they say there is some extra power. So I ask 'em where is it at, the power?—and they tell me. I ask 'em how long it takes to get ready, the doctor and the nurses and the others? 'Oh,' they said, 'a couple of hours; maybe in an hour.' So I tell them I will let them know when it is to be and that I want everybody checked out and our own security, from the police, will stand guard over the power while it is going on. That's how it was, and the operation was a great success and nobody tried anything, and I thank the good Lord I am all right. What do the doctors know about these things? The doctors don't know anything."

On the surface, following the Democratic Convention in July, Daley was performing his mayoral duties with his usual dispatch. At a City Hall press conference on Monday, August 23, Alderman Michael Bilandic of Daley's 11th Ward presented at Daley's instigation a voluminous document containing the details of major ordinances enacted by the Chicago City Council in the first sixteen months of Daley's sixth four-year term. The legislation covered ninety-seven categories, ranging from adoption of a strict fire code for high-rise buildings to establishment of a city personnel system that virtually erased civil service and placed control in Daley's hands over the hiring and firing of all city workers. Bilandic crowed that the document established that "Our Council is the best and most effective legislative body in the country."

An anti-Daley administration alderman who chanced by, Martin J. Oberman of Paddy Bauler's disemboweled 43rd Ward, instantly challenged him. Bilandic, a naive-appearing fellow who had been chosen by Daley to be floor leader of City Council when Alderman Thomas E. Keane went off to federal prison on a conviction for having fleeced the city in a land scheme, was nonplussed when Oberman hooted that his claim was a farce.

"An outsider reading this report," Oberman declared, "would have to conclude that our City Council never does anything unless the Mayor snaps his fingers."

A study of Bilandic's report did in fact allow for no doubt that Daley was the prime mover in every ordinance that the Council approved, virtually every proposal of consequence to be introduced coming not from an alderman but from the Mayor. The only noteworthy exceptions to this rule in Bilandic's report of great work done were two ordinances that Daley, while approving, would have regarded as "dirty"—the first prohibiting operation of sexual massage parlors within the limits of Chicago, and the second imposing harsh criminal penalties on prostitutes caught working the city streets, these ordinances being introduced by Alderman Edward M. Burke of the 14th, who was spokesman for the administration in matters of this nature.

Asked for reply to Oberman's criticism that the City Council functioned almost exclusively at the whim of Daley, Bilandic conceded that every ordinance of any importance that passed had been introduced by Daley. He argued, however, that it was "part of his innovative genius that the Mayor doesn't introduce things unless they are plausible, beneficial, and workable."

Analysis of Mayor Daley's innovative genius would show that he excelled in searching out new sources of revenue and spending every dollar that the city could get its hands on. Thus it was that he instituted an increase in the city vehicle tax, boosting the city's take threefold to an impressive $42.9 million per year; that he increased the tax on household utility bills to an annual net of $129.2 million; that he fought for a share of the state sales tax that gave Chicago $92 million per year; that he cooperated in passage of a state income tax that contained a kickback to Chicago of $42.2 million a year.

An inherently cautious man, Daley had the political good sense to diversify his tax grabs when it appeared that increasingly high real estate levies, approaching the point of being oppressive, might bring him down.

Expanded powers of home rule had been Daley's priority interest in the rewriting in 1970 of the 1870 Illinois Constitution. In the limitations imposed for 100 years, the city of Chicago, with three and a half million population, had been prohibited from exercising its own judgment of what could be taxed. Under the 1870 Constitution, approval of the state legislature was required for the submission of general obligation bonds to referendum.

Home rule made it possible for Daley to require employers to pay the city three dollars per employee per month, a "head" tax that produced $28.5 million per year and prompted many firms to pack up and leave Chicago. Daley introduced a tax on cigarettes sold within the city, the annual return on this amounting to $17.5 million a year. He instituted a home-rule tax on automobile parking, amounting to $12.8 million a year.

With freshwater Lake Michigan at its doorstep, Chicago was able to turn a tidy profit on tapping this resource, chlorinating it, and getting it into the pipes. The cost of operating the water system in calendar 1977 was placed at $73.9 million, but Daley's 1977 budget anticipated water revenue of $121.2 million— reflecting an increase over 1976 of 21.5 percent in the rates. It was with many sly taxes that Daley had made "the city that works" work.

Not the least of the hidden taxes that Daley slipped onto the books was a 5-percent "occupational tax" that must be paid by the hotels and motels on all occupied accommodations. The take on this was variable, working out to several millions of dollars. Part of these proceeds were reserved for the promotion of tourism in Chicago, but the bulk of the money was spent at the discretion of Mayor Daley and a career promoter named Colonel Jack Reilly, who wears a patch over one eye, looking like a lean Irish pirate, and who served Daley as director of special events. According to a provision of the ordinance that created this tax, the city comptroller was required to make quarterly reports on expenditures to the City Council. The quarterly reports make fascinating reading, as witness:

City of Chicago
Municipal Hotel Operators Occupation Tax Fund
Statement of Expenditures
FOR THE THREE MONTHS ENDED DECEMBER 31, 1975

Monthly Contribution for the Promotion of Chicago Convention and Tourism	$180,475.00
Luncheon—Honoring Prince Bertil of Sweden	3,871.20
Christmas Parade	35,301.20
Chicago's Observance of the United States Bicentennial of the American Revolution	1,024.87
Lakefront Festival	13,142.78
Luncheon—Honoring Prime Minister of Tunisia	2,866.70
Reception—Chicago Consular Corps	4,971.27
Inauguration of the Mayor of Chicago and the City Council	6,462.65
Dinner—Honoring the President of the Federal Republic of Germany	114.50
Memorial Wreath for the Stephen A. Douglas Memorial	227.75
Reception—The Illinois Municipal League Conference	3,442.40

Luncheon—Honoring the Emperor and Empress of Japan	22,556.59
American Freedom Train Program	5,920.40
Contribution—Lyric Opera	100,000.00
Luncheon—Honoring Astronauts and Cosmonauts	15,276.13
Dinner—President Gerald Ford	2,240.25
Chicago Parade Flag Present to the Stockyards Kitty Band	29.32
Reception—Honoring the President of Iceland	1,367.30
Dedication of John C. Kluczynski Federal Building	5,141.00
Holiday Folk Fair	17,563.75
Dinner—Honoring His Excellency Anwar Sadat	22,573.02
Concert—University of Southern California in the Civic Center Plaza	1,135.00
Veterans' Day Observance	140.00
Graduation Ceremonies for the Navy	143.90
Operation Sail—Invitations for Foreign Sailing Ships to Visit Chicago	61.05
Official Breakfast—Lord Mayor of Dublin	374.54
Luncheon—Marine Drum and Bugle Corps	375.00
Luncheon—Tuley High School	174.50
Luncheon—Phillips High School	225.50
Luncheon—Mayor of Frankfurt, Germany	452.85
Reception—Mayors of Illinois	90.00
Dinner—Honoring Prime Minister of Israel Yitzhak Rabin	2,100.97
Honorary Citizens Medals and Medals of Merit to Distinguished Persons	1,480.00
Christmas Program—City Hall Lobby	55.00
	$451,376.39

In one way or another, the citizens of Chicago paid the price of having Mayor Daley pop up at a white-tie dinner to toast Her Royal Highness, the queen of Denmark ($5,229.00), or having him wax sentimental at a green-sash affair for His Excellency, the prime minister of Ireland ($19,118). No one in Chicago's City Hall ever explained the criteria that guided Daley's decision to lay out a spread for the president of Nicaragua, the king of Jordan, the prime minister of Israel; or why, oddly, he ignored the visits to Chicago of other dignitaries.

No explanation was offered as to why a film crew from Telefez Eireann was welcome in his office, and why a crew from the BBC was not. It was never revealed what Daley's judgments were on authorizing the expenditure of $44,309 for lakefront fireworks on the Fourth of July, $5,000 for the purchase of 65,000 coho salmon for Lake Michigan, a bequest of $25,000 for a livestock show, and small sums for the purchase of medals for show business people, who were grandly welcomed into his presence. In what manner any of this bolstered anything in Chicago, other than Daley's ego, was never explained. No one ever asked, actually, about the equity of big money's being tossed about on trivial display in a city that made no effort to house its poor and that defied the federal courts in the matter of discriminatory hiring practices on the part of its Police Department.

Self-aggrandizement apparently was the intent of Daley's clinking glasses with the high-and-mighty, trading quips with the Frank Sinatras and the Bob Hopes, holding a pose for news photographers as he raised a glass of bubbly in toast to the queen of Denmark or the president of Nicaragua. Lord knows the newspapers and television had hardly ever failed to run pictures of him splashing about in his celebrity pool.

Even when he had returned disheartened from the Democratic Convention in New York, 1976, the intermittent visitation of celebrities to his city and his throne continued in testimony that Daley was still an important man on his home grounds, and he appeared, no matter who got shoved aside as he snuggled into the limelight with a distinguished visitor, to regard being in the center of attention as his due.

Somewhat to the dismay of Democratic party people, who murmured among themselves that Daley was not attending to business, he had become so grasping for attention that he had lost his mystique. The Democratic party people were distressed that Daley did not seem to realize, or care, that his preoccupation with promoting himself was hurting the party candidates for county and state offices. The desire of Daley was to enhance his image as an exceedingly powerful politician; the error of his thinking was that large segments of the public now feared him— and even Republicans, who had consistently hailed him as a great mayor, voiced warning to each other over their coffee and brandies that it would be foolhardy to allow him, through thé election of Mike Howlett as governor, to take control of the state.

Howlett's identity with Daley was, he knew, the greatest handicap he could have. "It's the kiss of death to have a Daley connection," Howlett sighed. "You can't fight with him, or you're liable to lose Chicago. If you don't get his arm off your back, you're a cinch to lose outside of Chicago. Even if I could think of some way to have a fight with him, I'm not sure it would do me any good outside of Chicago—because I'm not sure the people would believe it was on the square.

"Take Carter," Howlett went on. "What is Daley telling the Carter people? 'You take care of Downstate and I'll take care of Chicago'—that's what he's telling them. Why shouldn't Daley be able to deliver in Chicago, for Cry sakes? We got a pretty good vote in Chicago for McGovern, for Cry sakes. We won here for Humphrey, in '68. Sure, Daley will give Carter a vote in Chicago—only a lot of the vote will come from Carter himself, him getting it in spite of Daley. But Daley will take the credit for Carter winning in Chicago and if Ford takes Illinois, Daley will sit back and tell the Carter people, 'Well, I thought you fellows were going to take care of the suburbs and Downstate.' He is a very strange man, Daley, only seeing things his own way."

At breakfast with Daley in advance of Jimmy Carter's first campaign visit to Chicago on September 9, Howlett was shaken up to discover that Daley, who was being lashed by Jim Thompson, Howlett's Republican opponent for governor, was visibly upset at the shots that Thompson was taking at him and apparently unconcerned about the damage that Thompson might be inflicting upon Howlett's chances for victory in November. "The only one Daley ever worries about," observed Howlett, "is Daley."

It had been Howlett's desire that Daley avoid direct involvement in his campaign. Howlett had feared that Thompson, from the beginning, had settled on the strategy that his best chance for victory lay in tarring Howlett with the brush of his Daley connection. The paradox of Daley's bipartisan reputation as the most able big-city mayor in the nation, nationally admired for his ability to run the only major city in the nation that "worked," was that Daley was regarded with great distrust by citizens of Illinois who resided outside of Chicago.

On the one hand, he was acclaimed as an efficient dictator whose word was law; on the other hand, there was widespread belief that Daley's ambition was to control all of the state as he controlled Chicago. A politically astute Democrat who had kept a distance between himself and Daley over the years, with a strong Downstate following of his own, Howlett had been hopeful if not confident that his independence of Daley would protect him from accusations that he was, in fact, Daley's puppet. And now here, two months in advance of the election, there was Daley launching an attack on Thompson that could only serve to confirm the suspicion that Mike was the dummy on Richard's knee. "He wasn't smart enough to stay out of it and let me handle Thompson in my own way," sighed Howlett.

At a September 7 meeting of the Democratic Central Committee at the Bismarck Hotel, supposedly called to firm up arrangements for Jimmy Carter's first campaign visit to Chicago two days later, Daley angrily attacked Thompson. Perhaps Daley was inspired to this by reports from throughout the state that Howlett was running an inept campaign; that Carter's people were openly discussing their fears that Howlett was dragging them down in Illinois; that the first public opinion polls indicated that Thompson had already assumed a lead and that his advantage over Howlett was broadening. It was possible that Daley had decided that something had to be done quickly to reverse this negative trend. Quite as likely, however, Daley was reacting to the taunting by Thompson that Howlett was nothing more than Daley's surrogate; that Howlett was slated as merely a front whereby Daley would extend his frightening power across the state, subjugating the interests of the Downstate people to his own dictates.

In fighting stance, waving a clenched fist at his committeemen, Daley portrayed Thompson as the hired gun of the United States Justice Department. Roaring and rambling, Daley snarled: "Nixon appointed him to be the United States attorney and the whole reason was to attack the Democratic party of Chicago. Does he forget, this Thompson, how he was appointed? As everybody knows, Thompson, what he did was use the immunity to get witnesses so he could make the headlines, indicting a great many innocent people with immunity testimony—and all you've got to do is look at the record and there is the proof!"

Reporters crowded around Daley to ask for comment on Thompson's charge that Daley was the real issue of the gubernatorial campaign, that Daley's intention was to run the state if he could get Howlett elected. With a look of disdain, Daley replied, "Maybe somebody should have been running something when Thompson was working for Mr. Mitchell, the attorney general, followin' orders and givin' this immunity to everybody over there, in return for the testimony. And why don't he explain what happened to his investigation of the vice-president, Mr. Agnew—who called him off of it and who told him to be quiet and Thompson doin' what his orders were?"

Within the hour, Thompson was responding. "Daley is lying," he declared. "He has his facts mixed up and he is lashing out at me because he knows that Howlett is going to lose because Howlett is Daley's candidate. The people of Illinois are fed up with Daley and his candidates. If he recalls, *I'm* the one who called Agnew a crook—and this was when Agnew was still vice-president and everyone was weeping tears for him.

"Daley as usual is twisting the truth; the only connection I had with the Agnew case, they called me to Washington to investigate leaks to the press in this case. But no one, including John Mitchell, gave me any orders regarding political corruption cases."

Wasn't it true that Thompson made a practice of granting immunity to people involved in bribery and conspiracy cases, in return for their testimony against elected officials? "There is no other way you can prove up a case," he answered, "other than by granting immunity to lesser defendants. The major defendants in all of these cases that we tried were elected officials who had violated the public trust and deserved to be prosecuted." Did Thompson have any regrets? "Yes, I regret that I secured immunity for John Daley in an extortion case against one of the Democratic county commissioners. John Daley is the mayor's cousin and one of his ward committeemen, and he made a poor witness; if I had that to do over again, I would not seek immunity for John Daley."

The Richard J. Daley Democrats turned out 100,000 strong to welcome Jimmy Carter to Chicago on the night of September 9. The candidate, who had made routine campaign appearances in Downstate Springfield and Peoria, got off to a discouraging start on his visit to the Chicago area, after alighting from his chartered United Airlines jet, "Peanut One," at Chicago's little-used Midway Airport. His motorcade had sped off to the southwestern suburb of Evergreen Park, at the request of Congressman Martin Russo (D., Ill.), who was struggling to be reelected—and Carter had been greeted by the protest of vocal anti-abortionists.

Transported thereafter to the Hyatt Regency Chicago Hotel, in the North Michigan Avenue area of downtown Chicago, Carter smiled broadly in response to applause from a crowd of perhaps one hundred who had gathered for his arrival. After a proper interval, Mayor Daley's car drove up and he was quickly taken to an elevator and on his way to a meeting with the candidate. This, Daley assured Carter, was to be a big night.

In Daley's tradition, a torchlight parade was the grand finale, the climax of a national campaign—always held on the weekend prior to the November election date. In 1976, with his own candidates foundering and Carter barely ahead of Ford in Illinois in the straw polls, Daley had advanced the date of the parade as a way of getting his machine off dead center. At meetings of his ward committeemen, Daley had exhorted them to get out the troops. His chief of parades, one-eyed Jack Reilly, had lectured the committeemen on the urgency for a big turnout. "It's not that the Mayor loves a parade, or that I love a parade," he declared; "the purpose of this parade is to focus attention of the people on this campaign."

The seventy-seven-year-old Reilly had a stolid audience for his exhortations: fifty ward committeemen, thirty committeemen from the Cook County townships outside of Chicago; William A. Lee, president of the Chicago Federation of Labor and his functionaries; Louis F. Pieck of the Teamsters and his people; Robert Johnston of the United Auto Workers; the Steel Workers, the Bricklayers, the Machinists, the Garment Workers, and so on. "Bodies!" the aging Reilly cried, in his twangy voice; "we want bodies! We want a hundred thousand in that parade—big floats and bands and everybody with horns! You'd be surprised how much noise you can get from a few horns on the back of a truck."

Mayor Daley had told reporters that the torchlight parade for Jimmy Carter would be "the finest salute to a candidate ever given in the history of the city of Chicago." The secret of a good parade, he said, was organization. "You get everybody to participate—the ward organizations, the labor, the citizens— You get the police to put up your barricades along the streets, so that people can stand behind and watch, and with the bands and the marchers you have a great parade." Daley had a great deal of faith in the voter productivity of parades. "You get a man interested enough to get in the parade—a man or a woman—and you've got a man or a woman that's interested in going out and talking to the neighbors about the candidates, and that's what it is, the torchlight parade—the beginning of the door-to-door campaign."

Daley produced a grand parade for Jimmy Carter. The Democrats and the union people turned out en masse, many of them carrying railroad flares and waving banners, ethnic groups in costume of their native lands, bands without number. Assembling at State Street and Wacker Drive, at the bridge, they went eastward to Michigan Avenue, then northward over the Chicago River to Ohio Street, then westward for one block to Medinah Temple on Wabash Avenue, about a mile from start to finish. Carter, riding in an open car with Daley and Senator Stevenson—Mike Howlett downgraded to a seat in a car back in the procession—smiled and waved, wearing the puzzled and delighted look of a child as Daley's orderly mob cheered him and a king's ransom of fireworks exploded safely above him, lighting up the sky.

Here and there, small bands of Pro Life demonstrators waved banners in protest, but Carter averted his eyes and Daley acted as if he were not aware, nudging the presidential candidate in the ribs occasionally and pointing out some of the more elaborate floats—the two extravagantly decorated CTA (Chicago Transit Authority) buses that the Amalgamated Transit Union had placed in the parade, and the proud banner of the float of the Lathers Union, proclaiming that Local 112 had been first among the organized labor groups of Illinois to endorse Jimmy Carter.

Carter appeared to regard Daley's presentation with genuine amazement. Senator Stevenson, uncomfortable in this setting, occasionally broke into a smile and waved a hand at the crowds gathered behind the barricades and passed a quick word with the presidential candidate, but mostly he looked bored. For his part, Daley sat firmly in his seat, flashing his public-appearance grin on and off in an automated way, raising his head and waving in recognition when he spotted someone who merited a gesture of attention—although mostly, Daley was the picture of an entrepreneur who had been through all of this many times before and was relieved to be going through it without anything untoward marring the show once again.

Alighting from the car at Medinah Temple, Daley kept at Carter's side as they hurried into the crowded hall for the anticlimactic finale of the Daley organization's spectacular. There were huge photographic blowups of Carter and Daley and Mondale and Howlett and Stevenson hanging in the background as the presidential candidate and his mayoral escort walked onstage; the special-privilege people who had received tickets for the rally filled the hall with cheers, Carter waving and showing all of his teeth, Daley pounding his hands together as if leading this throng in its applause.

Prior to the arrival of the stars of this extravaganza, a series of speakers had yammered to the noisy throng, assailing Gerald Ford's pardon of former President Nixon, castigating James R. Thompson as the toady of Nixon and the discredited former Attorney General John N. Mitchell, laboring the theme that only through the election of Carter and Howlett could the nation and the state get back on the pathway of solvency and salvation. This was all old stuff to the party faithful and hardly anyone had any interest in what was being said, as one speaker after another took a turn at trying to inspire enthusiasm among the manicured mechanics of the Daley machine. Periodically, someone would cheer or applaud and then others would do so, but the tedium of having to endure these feeble attempts at oratory was depressing. "All of these guys," a functionary of the First Ward organization observed to committeeman John d'Arco, "they are all flat as piss on a platter."

There was an awakening of interest as Daley marched in at the side of Jimmy Carter. Conceivably, Carter viewed this howling mob as having gathered in tribute to himself; he did not know, perhaps, that most would have preferred to be bellied up to a bar or be home watching television and that they were present only because they were under orders from Daley to be there—the Poles and the Slovenians, the Italians and the Lithuanians, the Irish, the blacks, and the Ukrainians.

The merciful part of the Daley machine rallies was that the speeches were short; a party leader was introduced, he waved in acknowledgment of the applause, he paid verbal tribute to The Great Mayor, he made his point, and he went back to his seat. Senator Stevenson's role was to speak to the question of party unity. There were brawny Democrats in the audience who would have cheerfully taken Governor Dan Walker into a dark alley to beat him up, but they dutifully applauded when Stevenson equated Walker and Carter, referring to them as being alike in their compassion for their fellow man and in sharing a dedication to the principles of the Democratic party.

There was audible booing when Walker was introduced, Daley glaring at the audience. Quite aware that he was facing the ward people who had produced the vote that beat him in the March 16 primary, Walker declared, a tone of defiance in his voice, "I am here tonight because I want to be here tonight." An apostate who had put his knee in the groins of both Howlett and Daley, disliked and distrusted by most of the crowd that had responded to his introduction with less than moderate applause, Walker waxed eloquent on the need to elect both Howlett and Carter. There was a detectable emphasis in his endorsement of Carter, not unobserved by the Democratic workers who sat listening to him. There was almost a sigh of relief in Medinah Temple when Dan Walker sat down.

Howlett was next. He thanked Walker. He praised Daley. He hailed Carter as a Democratic messiah. Then, reverting to his campaign themes, he denounced Jim Thompson as a "Nixon Republican," a political rookie, an opportunist who was trying to reap a political harvest from a field he had fertilized with the carcasses of "good men that he has destroyed." In conclusion, Howlett roared, "Let me tell you: On November 2nd, the Democrats of Illinois will have a great victory. I'll beat the pants off Thompson!" Great applause. There were few in the audience who were sanguine about Howlett's chances against Thompson. "Walker crapped all over him and ruint him," one of Vito Marzullo's aides had observed—but Mike Howlett had always been on the square with everyone, had been regarded as a politician of high integrity, until the Walker people set out to dirty him up, and Howlett was the sentimental favorite of the Daley people who had been turned out for the Carter rally, although regarded as doomed to lose in November.

The pragmatic Daley gamely referred to Walker as "our great Governor" as he started to speak, paid brief compliments to Mike Howlett, got in a mention of Senator Stevenson and each of the state candidates on the Democratic ticket, and then proceeded to shovel praise upon Jimmy Carter. Daley had known all along, he said, that Carter was a winner. "Even at the start of the great state primaries when nobody knew who Jimmy Carter was," his practiced eye had spotted Carter as the future candidate, the next president.

There was hardly a person in the hall who believed a word of this, everyone aware that Daley "wasn't too good" with Carter; even so, Daley could unashamedly lick boots when need be with the best of them, and his troops, while wryly amused at being witness to ass-kissing time in sweet Chicago, figured that Daley knew what he was doing and they were pulling for him to make a good impression on the man who seemed destined to be elected president.

When, as the main attraction, Jimmy Carter was introduced to Daley's people, everyone in Medinah Temple leaped to his

feet and the applause was quite loud. Carter appeared over-
whelmed by this reception and Daley seemed to be exploding
with pride. The crowd slowly settling back into its chairs, Carter
turned smilingly toward Daley and began his talk with several
minutes of compliments to the Mayor. Sitting with hands folded
in his lap, his head lowered in a show of modesty, Daley's face
flushed as Carter recounted the legends of the miraculously high
vote totals that Daley had produced for President John F.
Kennedy, President Lyndon B. Johnson, the vote that Daley had
delivered for Hubert Humphrey in 1968 and for George McGovern in 1972.

"Mayor Daley is a man who never lets you down," Carter
declared. "In good years and in bad, he makes a full effort for
any candidate of the Democratic party." He referred to Daley as
"my very good friend," and the crowd cheered. He spoke of the
great leadership that Daley had supplied the city of Chicago
over a span of twenty years, and the crowd cheered. Searching
for superlatives, Carter finally settled for the old line: "As is well
known through all of the nation, Chicago is the city that works,
and Mayor Daley is the man who sees to it that Chicago is the
city that works." Automatically, the crowd cheered.

Carter had put in a hard day of campaigning in Illinois. He
had fenced with the Pro Lifers in Springfield and Peoria and
had had a rather grim confrontation with them in suburban
Evergreen Park, finding it expedient to declare, "Abortion is not
just an issue with the Roman Catholics; there are a lot of Southern Baptists, Methodists, Lutherans, and other religious denomi-
nations that don't think abortion is right." To balance his concession with those who might think otherwise, Carter had said,
"There are a lot of Catholics who are not for a constitutional
amendment on abortion. It's a mistake for us to think this is a
church issue."

It angered Daley that abortion was an anti-Carter issue.
"What has this got to do," he had asked Howlett, "on whether
someone should be president?" Daley was bitter over reports
that John Cardinal Cody was reported, on the very day that
Carter was in Chicago, to be launching an anti-abortion voter
protest in the archdiocese. Pro Life advocates were directing let-

ters to Daley, accusing him of sacrificing his religious beliefs on the altar of political expediency. Copies of some letters were being sent to the media—some of the letters accusing Daley of committing a sacrilege when, refusing to stand with Mother Church on the issue of protecting the unborn, he continued to approach the rail to receive Holy Communion. When Carter verbalized on the question of abortion, Daley pursed his lips, looked guilty, and said nothing.

Abortion classified with Richard Daley as a "dirty" campaign issue; even oblique references to abortion embarrassed him. He seemed to believe he had been trapped on the wrong side of a moral question and privately, it was said, Daley was troubled. Mike Howlett had stated his anti-abortion position with no hesitation—telling his aides, "If I get pounded for it, I'll just have to take whatever the heat is; Daley thinks he can bullshit this thing through with Cody, pretending it isn't a problem. Crissakes, even Carter says people feel very deeply about it."

The Daley machine Democrats who had gathered in Medinah Temple to impress Carter were, in fact, uninterested in the turmoil over abortion; it didn't matter to them that there was a right-to-life picket line outside the hall, or that Daley might be fearful that, in compromising his lifelong acceptance of all churchly teaching, he might be in jeopardy of losing his immortal soul.

As a practicing politician, Daley had reason to doubt that the abortion question would translate into an anti-Carter vote on election day; as a practicing Catholic, Daley had reason for remorse that His Eminence, Cardinal Cody, was reproving him in ecclesiastic letters that were being sent to all parishes of the Chicago archdiocese. Having held throughout his life in politics that every man is accountable for his own actions, having been mortified at various times by disclosure of the transgressions of politicians who had exerted influence upon his career, Daley folded his arms and defied the accusing finger that a prince of his church seemed intent upon pointing at him.

It was with relief that Mayor Daley jumped to his feet in Medinah Temple, as candidate Carter came to the end of a half-hour speech that had broken Daley's rule of "keep it short."

Pumping Carter's hand, as Carter waved his other hand in acknowledgment of the applause coming from a crowd that was already working its way toward the exits, Daley appeared eager to be escorting the presidential candidate out of the place—anxious to get him into a limousine and send him on his way to the hotel, Daley then getting into his own limousine and heading for his bungalow on South Lowe Avenue in Back-of-the-Yards Bridgeport. Daley looked tired and sad rather than ebullient, although he knew that he had accomplished all that he could have hoped to accomplish, showing Jimmy Carter that when it came to putting it on for a man running for president, there was no one who could equal the efforts of the reliable Dick Daley.

With Carter flying off at once to Milwaukee, Wisconsin, the excitement engendered by his campaign visit to Chicago vanished. Daley remained confronted by a steady flow of mail that accused him of cowardice in refusing to "speak out in defense of life, on the abortion issue." He received many letters that charged him with a denial of his faith: "We are shocked by your refusal to speak out on the great moral issue of our age. We are sickened and disillusioned that you put the Democratic party ahead of God Almighty."

On the day following Carter's big day in Chicago, Daley's press secretary, Frank Sullivan, revealed that a letter of reply was being sent over the Mayor's signature to persons who had reviled him for his refusal to oppose Carter on the abortion question. Reversing his position that abortion was not a significant election issue, Daley's letter said: "My comment that it was not an important issue was a mistake. I frankly admit that it is not what I intended to say." The letter then went on to declare, "I will work for a constitutional amendment to override the Supreme Court opinion on abortion."

Democratic politicians, learning of this letter, grunted, some observing that Daley had waited until Carter was safely out of sight before revealing that he had had a change of mind. Even so, Daley had been rebuked by a mild statement of Cardinal Cody that, while the Cardinal had never urged people to vote for or against a particular candidate or party, "I am obliged to speak out on moral and ethical issues that often are at the heart of political positions." And it was believed that, with Cody holding that it was "the right of the people to seek a constitutional amendment," Daley could not hold otherwise. As Daley wavered, there was fear expressed by many of Daley's committeemen that the abortion issue would cost them votes on election day, two months hence—although Alderman Vito Marzullo, the feisty old-time boss of the preponderantly Democratic 25th Ward, sneered in his tough Sicilian accent, "In my community, nobody pays any attention to this Cardinal Cody or any pope. Let them run their church and we will run the politics."

As if trying to get away from his troubles, Daley was discovered to be slipping out of his home on South Lowe Avenue with increasing frequency in the pre-dawn hours of subsequent September mornings. His curtain-peeking Bridgeport neighbors, alert to every sign of activity outside the Daley bungalow, were at first mystified to observe the Mayor, who prided himself on never appearing in public without jacket and tie, come striding down the sidewalk to his limousine in checkered sports shirt and slacks.

More of these mornings than not, they saw him return a couple of hours later, quick-stepping up the walk to the side entrance of his brick home, trailed by a plainclothes bodyguard with a shimmering Chinook salmon balanced in his hands. Daley was plainly delighted when reporters discovered his secret, but firmly refused the pleadings of photographers that they be allowed to tag along. A fisher for the votes of men, who observed few limits in seeking to land his catch, Daley explained that fishing for fish was something that required a degree of privacy.

"I like to get out there, off McCormick Place, about five o'clock—before your 'gentlemen fishermen' in their fancy boats are out there. What happens, it takes the bait, the salmon runs when he's caught. What you do—there are other boats around you, you holler, 'Fish! Fish!' and all of those other boats get out of your way. The fish like to go under the boats, to get away, so it can't be too crowded out there. Sometimes, you know, you haven't got it hooked right and he runs off the line."

The captain of the chartered boat that Daley used, Sam Romano, said that not too many Chinook got off Daley's line. "He's one of the most patient fishermen I've ever seen, Daley is. He'll play a fish for an hour, if that's what it takes to land it." Daley declared that Romano, who took his fleet to Florida waters in the winter season, had assured him that Chicago "is the salmon-fishing capital of the world. It's the best in Chicago right now. They're coming into Burnham, Diversey, and all the other great harbors. Belmont. Every place."

On Friday, September 17, when Peggy Lee, a singer who was filling an engagement in Chicago, was escorted by a press agent into Daley's office, Miss Lee was good enough to smile when she was upstaged by a Polaroid picture of a nineteen-pound fish that the Mayor said he had caught that very morning off McCormick Place. "There were fifty to sixty boats out there today," Daley said, "and while I got the fish, I watched the sun come up in the east and saw Chicago's beautiful skyline, from out there in the lake." With a grin on his face, Daley showed his picture, proudly holding his catch.

"I took this one home and cleaned it and I stuffed it, and Mrs. Daley will cook it and tonight we will have our dinner, right out of our lake." Sometimes, Daley said, he did the cooking. "You got to clean 'em and spread on the mayonnaise, so's he won't dry out on you. Then you cook it slow in the oven for about three hours and then you put it on a wooden plate and cover with the hot sauce and it is food for a king."

A few days later, on September 22, Daley proved to be uncommunicative. Besieged by reporters for comment on the disclosure that Jimmy Carter had confessed to *Playboy* magazine that he had "committed adultery in his heart many times" and that he had "looked on a lot of women with lust," Daley was stone-faced and turned away. Alderman Mike Bilandic of Daley's ward was indignant that the press would badger the Mayor with such questions as this. "The Mayor is too busy with the budget to comment on Carter and sex," Bilandic declared. Even the uninhibited Vito Marzullo declined to express his thoughts on Carter's adventurous remarks to *Playboy*. "I'm in the politics business, not the sex business," he said. "I had nine children and nineteen grandchildren and the record speaks."

Finally, on September 24, Daley took the baited question. After responding repeatedly to the Carter interview question with a sneering response, "What do *you* think?" Daley chuckled and suggested to the City Hall reporters who gathered around him that they take a poll among themselves as to what public reaction to Carter's candid comments might be. "Add up the poll," he said, "and then you can give me the results." When reporters replied that their opinions were not important, that he, not they, had the political wisdom to assess the damage that Carter might have done his campaign, Daley laughed and said, "Me? I'm just a kid from the Stockyards."

Thereupon, Daley pulled out another picture of himself and a fish; this one, he said, had been a twenty-five-pounder. Innocently, a reporter asked, "What did the fish think of the *Playboy* interview?" The Mayor was momentarily perplexed by the question. Then, smiling broadly, he replied, "He said he wouldn't have got caught if he had kept his mouth shut," and, chortling, the Mayor hustled back to his office.

Daley's willingness to be witty about Carter's confession to *Playboy* about a "bunch of women" getting screwed seemed out of character with the good-family-man image that Daley had always strived to cultivate. It appeared to Daley watchers that, like Carter, the Mayor was not immune to periodic attacks of slack jaw, but those who knew him best could not understand what had prompted Daley, after several days of silence, to joke about Carter's recital of having wrestled with carnal temptations. It was quite uncharacteristic of Daley to speak to such a question as this—rather shocking, also, in the view of many of his admirers. What was the matter with Daley, they wondered, making a joke about sex?

Perhaps Daley was feeling worldly because he had secretly circumvented a trap that the Internal Revenue Service had been attempting to set for him. It was one of the secrets of Daley's private life that the IRS had culminated a study of his personal net worth with a request for a face-to-face discussion of his holdings. Daley had been furious when he discovered that he was the subject of investigation, placing the blame for this upon Jim Thompson, the former United States attorney who had put

Judge Otto Kerner, Alderman Thomas Keane, Alderman Paul Wigoda, and so many others in prison. Daley seemed to believe that he had been placed under investigation by friends of Thompson who were still in charge of the federal prosecutor's office.

The closest brush Daley had had with being accused of corruption had been the disclosure that he had personally directed that millions of dollars of city insurance be transferred to an Evanston firm, Heil & Heil, that had employed one of his boys. Even his good friend Dr. Oldberg blanched at that. "My opinion was that Daley was personally honest," Oldberg said, when interviewed after Daley's death, "but that Heil & Heil thing—that was as close to being 'far off' as I had known Dick Daley to be. It was a raw piece of business and I suppose the only explanation was that Dick was always trying to help his kids. I must say, though, that I didn't like it the least bit, and none of my friends liked it."

In speaking to the same question, Mike Howlett had said, "There was no doubt about it; he wanted to make some money for his kids. Parky Cullerton, who was county assessor, and George Dunne, who was president of the County Board, were mad as hell about it; they were in the insurance business, too, and the business that Daley gave to his kid, he took from them. It was like the law business he swung to his two kids who were lawyers, taking it from other fellows to give to the kids. When it came to helping the kids, Daley's attitude seemed to be, 'Somebody's kids are gonna get it; why not mine?"

There was a revival of gossip about the Daley kids when, on August 9, about one month after the Democratic Convention, federal Judge William J. Lynch died. Unconscious when discovered on the floor of his apartment early in July, Lynch had died without regaining consciousness, Mayor Daley, who had paid one visit to his old friend's bedside, issued the automatic statement of condolences: "All of Chicago is saddened. I have lost a very dear personal friend." Dr. Oldberg expressed a private opinion that Daley had "given up" on the judge, that Lynch had "sunk himself with his drinking" as far as the Daleys were concerned and that they had come to regard him as a lost cause.

But it had not been Judge Lynch's habit of drink that touched off the gossip, but rather the question of who got the several millions of dollars that Lynch had accumulated. Having started out in the practice of law with Dick Daley, Lynch had certainly done well. With no family to speak of, it was widely believed that he had left his money to the Daley kids. He left an unspecified sum in a trust and his brief will did not name his beneficiaries, but the gossip was that the Daley kids had been taken care of, as per a supposed arrangement of long standing between Daley and himself.

Widely held to be, personally, a dollar-honest mayor, Daley was worldly in his judgment of people in politics using their clout to make big money. He was tolerant of politicians who waxed rich on what is called "honest graft"; law business or real estate deals, for instance, that sprang out of political soil. Daley's rationale seemed to be that it takes money to be in politics and that everybody gets a little something here and there; so long as you were not involved in deals that were illegal or immoral, what was wrong with making some money when you had a good chance?

Disclosure that someone prominent in politics had been flopping around on the mattresses with girls was something else again. Daley was certain that a man could lose his immortal soul doing that. The distinction to be made, therefore, in the matter of politicians' obeying the Ten Commandments, was that it is realistic to make some money out of high position if you can, but reproachable to spend it in fulfillment of carnal desire. In the case of politicians who were practicing Catholics, going to confession on a regular basis, when they exhibited affluence beyond any definable source, there would seem to be a moral contradiction. But if you pressed the point of how they rationalized the taking of honest graft, you might be told with a knowing wink about a legendary priest who admonished politicians in his confessional that he wasn't interested in hearing them talk about their business—only their sins. Daley seemed to know the difference.

In the final month of his life, on December 2, 1976, eighteen days before he died, Daley had cried out in a speech against the commonly held belief that all politicians are venal. Speaking to the Illinois Association of County Officials, Daley lamented the low opinion that the public had of its political servants. He declared that everyone in public life in the modern day was "doubly suspect" of corruption, and he laid the blame for this on "reformers."

Defending his own integrity, Daley had said, "I've been in politics for forty-five years and there is not a man or woman in this state or nation who has ever corrupted me.

"Many of them have tried it," he declared. "But you know and I know that if I had been corrupted years ago, I wouldn't still be around."

Inevitably, there had been speculation across the years as to whether Daley had managed to pocket sizable sums of money. The closest anyone ever came to determining his net worth was election year 1976 when the Internal Revenue Service shocked Daley with a demand that he submit to an audit. It was ironic that Daley, who had a network of informants supplying him with details on the private life of everyone in whom he had an interest—who was gambling, who was drinking, who was playing around with women; there was not a single department or office in city government that did not have a Daley spy from the 11th Ward—zealously guarded the privacy of his own affairs. It was widely assumed that Judge Lynch, his original law partner, had intimate knowledge of Daley's finances; indeed, it was a longtime rumor in Chicago that Lynch was the overseer of funds that had mutually accrued to them.

Mary Mullen, who served Daley as personal secretary from the earliest days of his career, undoubtedly could have supplied some details of Daley's fortunes. She was once described as "probably the only living person who knows everything about Daley," having been his secretary when he was state director of revenue under Governor Adlai E. Stevenson in the 1940s. Fiercely loyal to the bitter end, Ms. Mullen was likewise tight-lipped and revealed nothing about Daley, even when he eased her out of Democratic headquarters into a job at City Hall—on the pretext that she needed to put in time to get her city pension. An informed observer, feeling sad about the downgrading of Mary, explained, "You see, as the Daley kids got older, they kept taking over more and more, advising their Dad more and more—especially Michael, the lawyer, who is the second son. Mary Mullen just didn't fit into their plans. So, gradually, she got eased out."

She had reason to retaliate, but it was extremely doubtful that Mary Mullen cooperated with the IRS when Daley was being checked out in 1976. She would have been a possible source of information; whatever there was to be known of Richard J. Daley's financial position, she knew. But it didn't figure that she would have talked.

To a somewhat lesser degree, this would also have been true of former Alderman Thomas E. Keane. For most of the first twenty years that Daley was mayor of Chicago, Keane was the leader of the City Council, in close association with Daley. There had not been a solitary piece of Council business, in those two decades, that was not personally scrutinized and approved by Tom Keane. He and Daley were not personal friends; but they would lavish praise upon each other at public functions— and Daley was surprisingly at pains to be gracious to Keane, during the period of his conviction on fleecing the city of tax foreclosure deals and the exhaustion of his court appeals.

At least in "ball park" figures, the canny Keane would have known the totals of the enormous amounts of money that had been in personal control of Daley, as Mary Mullen would have known, down through the years. Keane would have known, for example, that from the time that Daley became party chairman in 1953, Daley had been in complete charge of party funds. During a period of more than two decades, Daley had control of the proceeds of thirty or more $100-per-plate fund-raising dinners, each of them turning in a net profit of $500,000 or more.

Keane would have known that in this period, exclusive of campaign contributions of millions more that he did not have to account for, some $15 million was in personal control of Richard J. Daley—with Daley having to account to no one, other than the IRS. Only Daley knew how much he had in these accounts; only he had authority to spend it.

Until new state laws required a public accounting, starting in

1975, of all political funds, the report to be made in a sworn statement with the names of all major contributors listed, perhaps $30 million was in sole control of Chicago's "dollar-honest" Mayor. No one in Chicago ever challenged Daley to make an accounting of these enormous sums. Hardly anyone gave a thought as to how much money had passed in and out of Daley's hands, or what precisely he had done with any of it; Tom Keane would have been one of the few who thought about it, but it would have been a condition of his political accommodation with Daley that not even privately would he have challenged Daley to let him have a look at the books. Keane was therefore in a safe condition, having no information, to parry any questions IRS might put to him regarding the details of Daley's financial affairs. At the time in 1976 that IRS agents met with Daley to interrogate him, Tom Keane was in prison—serving five years on various counts of having used his control of the Chicago City Council to secure title to tax-delinquent property, concealing from the other aldermen his financial interest in these transactions. Keane was available for interrogation, but would hardly have talked.

No one, indeed, was likely to have talked, but Daley was nervous, as anyone might be, on the day appointed for his confidential meeting with IRS agents. By agreement, the inquiry was to be conducted in the offices of a well-known defense attorney named Harry J. Busch, directly across LaSalle Street from City Hall. Daley was seated in Busch's private office, arms folded and grim, as two IRS agents walked in. Daley had confided to Busch his fear that the government was trying to get something on him. "They are out to crucify me," he complained, "because they hate the Democrats."

Not a man to volunteer any secrets of his business, much less any possible sins, Daley had provided the lawyer with merely a sketchy accounting of the various dinner and campaign funds that he had controlled, leaving it up to Busch to get him out of the investigation of what had happened to the money. His planning complicated by a distinguished client who would not trust him with the information needed for a defense, Busch nonetheless had employed a strategem that he hoped would knock the

IRS off balance. No sooner had the agents taken seats than a court reporter with a stenotype machine entered the office through a side door.

"What is this?" the agents inquired. "This is our court reporter," Harry Busch replied; "it is my intention to have a transcript of every word that is spoken in this room." This is a defensive trick that is rarely resorted to except in cases in which the subject of a tax investigation is in serious criminal jeopardy. Since this was a routine audit of Daley's finances, the agents were aghast. "You can't do that," they argued. "Oh, yes, we can," Busch responded. One agent thereupon said he had better go to another office and telephone his supervisor, and Busch cooed that this would be the thing to do. Shortly, the agent was back and, with a wry look at his partner, he announced that they were leaving. They might return at a later date to make their interrogation, although they never did, but for the present a crisis in Richard Daley's life had been averted. And the agents never returned.

It was not only the government but Democratic party candidates as well who aggravated Daley over money matters, as the 1976 campaigns came closer to election day. There was muttering within the party leadership that Edward J. Egan's campaign for state's attorney of Cook County was foundering, for failure of Daley to fund it properly. Daley had persuaded the able Egan to resign as judge of the Appellate Court to make the race, the quid pro quo being that Daley would provide the votes and money. This, Daley did not do; indeed, when Daley died, the party organization had to assume an Egan campaign deficit of roughly $150,000.

In Mike Howlett's case, Daley had been even more penurious; again, having promised Howlett half a million dollars, he did not deliver it.

"I'm sorry to say that Daley seemed to lose interest in my campaign for governor, after I beat Dan Walker in the primary," Howlett said. "Before the primary, at a meeting in his office, he told me that he had a half a million that he'd cover me for," Howlett said, "but he never gave it to me. We raised all the money on our own, for the primary. All I ever got from Daley was $11,000. I thought he would start to help us after the primary, but I could see that there wasn't the same interest in me after the primary as he had had before. Daley pretty much took the attitude, after the primary, that he had already won what he wanted—when I knocked Walker out of the box.

"It wasn't so bad, his not giving us any money, but he hurt us by shutting off contributions on me real early—even before it looked like I wasn't doing too well. A fellow would come in to Daley and say, 'I want to give a little help to Mike,' and Daley would say, 'Never mind about Mike; give it to us—we need it here in the organization.' These fellows were telling Daley that they wanted to help me, because they wanted to score some points with him. But he put them in a box, telling them to give the contributions to him.

"I suppose Daley figured I would never know, but these fellows I'm talking about were friends of mine who go back a long way and so they told me that Daley was grabbing my contributions. So I knew—snap!—that quick, that he was shutting me off. I don't know why he would do that, so early, when there was no way of knowing how I would do in the election. Maybe he was trying to build up a pot to get out the vote for Carter, but he didn't seem to spend much on the election of Carter, either."

In late autumn of 1976, with the campaigns heating up, Howlett took a little shot at Daley. During an interview on Channel 11, the Public TV station in Chicago, Howlett was asked by political commentator Joel Weisman if there really was any particular point on which he was in disagreement with Daley. Howlett said, "Sure, there is; on money. Daley has given me only eleven thousand and he gave Walker fifty-five thousand. I'm supposed to be Daley's man and Walker has always been against him; but Walker got Daley's money and I haven't."

Next day, Howlett got a phone call from Daley. Characteristically, Daley made no admission that he had received word of what Howlett had said on television. "All he said," Howlett reported, "was that I shouldn't be worried about the money. I told him times were getting tough and Daley said, 'Well, you go ahead; there isn't any worry about the money. We'll cover you, after it's over.' The trouble was, he never covered me, before or after, which is why I ended up the campaign owing three hundred thousand."

Highly placed Democrats who thought themselves sensitive to Daley's moods, and knowledgeable people in the media who prided themselves on their ability to interpret his maneuverings, were similarly astonished at Daley's apparent lack of involvement in the campaigns of his state and county candidates. In the case of Judge Egan, not only did Daley withhold campaign funds, hobbling Egan's campaign for state's attorney; he tossed away a valuable endorsement that conceivably might have made the difference between winning and losing.

Chicago Tribune executives, disenchanted with four lackluster years of an incumbent state's attorney named Bernard Carey, a Republican, invited Daley to an off-the-record conference. The *Tribune* people had dropped a hint to Daley that they were displeased with Carey, thought highly of Egan, and were considering throwing the *Tribune*'s support to Daley's Democratic candidate. Totally misreading the intentions of the editorial and management bosses of the solidly Republican newspaper, Daley had walked into the meeting with a look of distrust and had quickly got into a diatribe against the press.

The *Tribune* people listened in disbelief, having done not the slightest thing to inspire this attack.

Privately advised by a source at the *Tribune* as to the purpose of the invitation to Daley, Mike Howlett was appalled when, having breakfast with Daley a few mornings later, Daley crowed to him about how he had "told off those guys at the *Tribune*." Later, in confidential conversation with his aides, Howlett recounted his breakfast talk with Daley and said, "My God, if he is doing so much damage to Egan—what is he doing to me?"

In fact, Daley was doing nothing overtly to hurt Howlett; he was merely keeping a distance from his candidate for governor. He had made only a token gesture of defense when Dan Walker had been cutting Howlett to ribbons on the matter of conflicts of interest. Although Mike had spelled out to Daley his outside business connections during the long period when Daley was trying to persuade him to be the candidate, Daley's judgment had been that not even the desperate Walker people would stoop to using this against Howlett. Daley was silent when they did. The Mayor had flippantly brushed aside questions, when asked about the anxiety of Carter and Mondale to avoid public appearances with Howlett—apparently fearful that the negative swell against him would engulf the national ticket. "They think he's a great candidate, Howlett," said Daley, lying boldly, aware that those in the Carter camp were fearful that the vote against Howlett would cost them the state of Illinois.

When Jim Thompson, the Republican party candidate for governor, hammered away at the theme "A vote for Mike Howlett is a vote for Dick Daley!" non-Chicago voters shivered in their shoes as Daley seemingly glowed with pride, many people believing that the threat of a Daley takeover must be true. Indeed, instead of helping Howlett escape the trap of a Daley connection, Daley seemed committed to portraying him as dancing when Daley worked the strings. In a familiar Daley phrase, if people wanted to regard Daley as the big man in the Democratic party of Illinois—"What's wrong with that?"

At no time, Howlett said, did Daley suggest strategy to counter the damaging Thompson charge that Downstate Illinois was in peril of being taken captive by the Chicago machine, and that this was what the election was all about. "He would holler back when Thompson attacked him, personally," Howlett said, "but it didn't bother him when Thompson was attacking me."

Daley professed to reporters that, contrary to what Thompson was thundering Downstate, he was not running Howlett's campaign. This was true, except that Daley persistently interjected himself into the campaign, sometimes with unfortunate results for Howlett. At a luncheon meeting of his ward and township organization members, for example, Howlett having left the room for another engagement, Daley introduced Anton Kerner, son of the late Judge Otto Kerner, who launched into a bitter attack on Thompson. Not only did young Tony accuse Thompson of having conspired to put his father in prison; he charged him with involvement in a plot of President Richard Nixon and Attorney General John Mitchell to destroy the Daley machine. Daley applauded young Kerner and thereafter, treating the allegation as if it were gospel, encouraged the idea that destruction of Richard J. Daley was a priority concern of the Nixon White House.

Next day, before Howlett could disengage himself from an issue that was certain to do him great damage, young Kerner went before a luncheon meeting of Young Democrats in Downstate Peoria and played a taped interview with Charles Colson, former special counsel to President Nixon, in which Colson spoke of a strategy meeting in Nixon's study at Key Biscayne, Florida, and quoted Mitchell as saying, "The Daley organization won't be so powerful when the grand jury gets through with them."

Having assented to the starting of this attack on Thompson, Daley clammed up to the point of not wishing to discuss it with Howlett. Bruised by Thompson's angry counterattack that Daley was engaging in "desperate, gutter politics," Howlett ridiculed Thompson, saying, "He doesn't have anything else to talk about and he doesn't understand state government, so he spends all his time running against Dick Daley." Privately, Howlett was bitter. "Daley," he said, "is the greatest politician Chicago ever had when it comes to taking care of himself, but he doesn't have much of a record for taking care of anyone else."

During their infrequent meetings, in the Mayor's office or over poached eggs and toast at the hotel headquarters of the party, Howlett, aware that Daley knew his campaign was foundering, sought to elicit from Daley an opinion of what might be done to turn things around. Later, Howlett complained to his top staff people that Daley was evasive. "I ask him for ideas, and he says, 'Just keep doin' what you're doin'.' I tell him that the straw polls that we are taking don't look too good, and he says, 'We'll get out a good vote for you.' I ask him about the Carter people treating me like I was poison and Daley says, 'Well, they're worried about Ford.'"

Howlett was aggravated by reports of the ward and township committeemen who passed information to him that they were getting telephone calls from Daley, exhorting them to get out a retention vote for Circuit Court Judge Joseph Power. Power was the 11th Ward associate of Daley who had been slated to run for a vacancy on the Illinois Supreme Court, only to suffer a humiliating defeat in the March 16 primary. Daley's nomination of Power had been a slap in the face of the substantial bloc of Polish voters in Chicago, who deeply resented Daley's refusal to choose a Pole to take the place of retiring Justice Thomas Kluczynski. There was likewise resentment against Power in the black community, by reason of Power's having throttled an investigation of the celebrated raid on the Black Panthers in December 1969, in which two well-known leaders of the militant group had been shot dead by detectives assigned to the Democratic state's attorney, Edward V. Hanrahan. In any event, not all the wizardry of the Daley machine could manage to get Joe Power nominated to run for the Supreme Court—and now, under a statute that required judges of the Circuit Court seeking retention to get a 60-percent vote of confidence at the end of their terms, Daley's Bridgeport pal was struggling to keep his seat on the bench. It was almost unprecedented for a Cook County judge to be voted down, but there was a widespread disenchantment with Power's fitness to remain as judge and he was in trouble. Responding to tips that a big vote for Power help top priority with Daley, Howlett was disgusted. "He isn't doing anything for me or the state ticket. He isn't doing anything to get Ed Egan elected state's attorney. But there is Daley, breaking his ass for Joe Power!"

Howlett's Republican opponent, Jim Thompson, taunted Howlett over Daley's manipulation of candidates for the judiciary. In an obvious shot at Daley's extraordinary effort to protect Joe Power's job, Thompson sneered, "The Democrats talk about 'judicial merit selection,' but the only merit system that the Cook County Democrats believe in is picking judges that Mayor Daley thinks have merit." In reply, Howlett snapped that, "Yeah, as Thompson can tell you, with the Downstate Republicans it's different. The Downstate Republicans select judges after they talk it over with God and the newspaper publishers. The newspaper coverage of this campaign is so distorted, state and national, if they dare me and Carter to walk across the Chicago River and we do it, they put out stories that this proves we don't know how to swim."

Thompson was careful to avoid confrontation with the sardonic Howlett, who might cut him down like a scythe. They had been personal friends and Thompson knew that there was little substance to his charge that Mike was Daley's puppet. It is nonetheless the accepted strategy of politics that you use every available weapon to win elections and Thompson was relentless in his warnings—speaking preacher-style in the black ghettos and in a red-neck drawl Downstate—that if the voters of Illinois weren't careful, Daley would get his grip on the throat of the entire state.

Throughout all the years that Richard J. Daley had been mayor, extolled by even conservative Republicans for his ability to make Chicago a city that "worked," political pundits had pondered the puzzle of why these admirers had held to the principle that he was not to be trusted beyond the limits of his city. The answer to this anomaly might be discovered perhaps in the conclusion reached half a century ago by a highly astute political writer for the Hearst newspapers, William H. Stuart.

Long before Daley came on the scene, Stuart had written that a gifted Chicago mayor would have the wholehearted support of the press and the business community—so long as he refrained from getting involved in state and national affairs. Daley would not have admitted to any such limitations on his acceptability, but displays of resistance to him—Republican enthusiasts invariably digging in to block the election of his state and national candidates—argue that not even Daley could escape obedience to old Bill Stuart's law. Defying the law of limited domain was nonetheless a compulsive thing on Daley's part. He was addicted to the delights of political power and, like any addict, he appeared in the elections of 1976 to have needs that were insatiable.

As if compelled to harvest the last grain of aggrandizement from his Illinois turf, Daley seemed intent upon creating an impression that the political fate of Howlett and Carter was in his hands. In the massive parade for Carter, at every huge precinct captain luncheon for Howlett, Daley exuded a possessive confidence that seemed to suggest it was with his personal approval that these men were candidates for public office. As a practical politician, Daley had to know that this image of a subservient connection with him translated beyond the corporate limits of his city into a probable loss of votes for the candidates. Yet, he seemed to thrust from his mind any suspicion he might have had that Howlett and Carter appeared to be struggling to keep their distance while sharing the limelight with him.

Perhaps Daley was not aware that the candidates knew the risks of being associated with him. He certainly knew that Carter's people were aware—because it had been persistently reported in the newspapers—that Downstate Democratic chairmen were in despair over what the Daley connection was doing to Mike Howlett. The chairman of populous Winnebago County, for example, where the vote had gone four to one for Governor Walker over Howlett in the March primary, was widely quoted two weeks prior to the November 2 election as saying, "The dislike for Mayor Daley is so great around here, it is killing us."

Walker was making little effort to redeem his pledge that he would campaign for Howlett; he ignored invitations to speak in many counties where he had run well in the primary, and made only perfunctory mention of Howlett's name at Democratic meetings that he did attend. At one meeting, someone asked Dan Walker if he honestly believed that Mike Howlett was his own man, and not the captive of Daley. Walker mugged a grin and turned to wink at an aide who was with him, before he looked at the questioner and said "Yes."

Having declared that he would campaign for Howlett in the interests of party unity, and in order that he could persuade those who had supported him to vote for Carter, Walker spoke principally in behalf of candidates for county office, who conceivably could help him in the political comeback he was expected to try to make two years later. When Walker's press secretary, Norton Kay, was asked if there would be joint appearances of Walker and Howlett in the closing days of the campaign, Kay replied that he didn't think so. "They would be pitted against each other by reporters. Walker would be asked how he could support a man who called him a sonofabitch in the primary."

The zealous amateurs who were striving to stack up enough

votes in Downstate Illinois to carry the state for Jimmy Carter were distressed by the undertones of the synthetic truce between the Daley and Walker forces. The public opinion polls showed that the advantage that Carter had held over Ford in Illinois at the start of the campaign had wasted away. The inexperienced people who were running Carter's Downstate campaign were not so naive that they did not realize that Howlett, pilloried by Walker and discredited by his Daley connection, was down the toilet.

The dilemma was that while Carter clearly would have to strike a neutral posture toward Daley in campaigning Downstate, he must look to be joyful while campaigning with Daley at his side in Chicago. To offset the losses that his association with Daley created Downstate, his chances of winning the precious twenty-six electoral votes of Illinois seemed clearly to depend upon Daley's ability to get him a plurality in Chicago of about 500,000 votes.

In past elections, Daley had produced such miracles as this. In 1960, in the face of religious prejudice against Roman Catholic John F. Kennedy, he had managed somehow to produce a plurality of 456,000—a performance that made possible Kennedy's 8,800-vote victory over Richard M. Nixon, with more than four and a half million votes cast in Illinois. But Kennedy had not been handicapped by a gubernatorial running mate like Howlett, who was doomed; Kennedy, on the contrary, had had the advantage of being on the ticket with the highly popular Judge Otto Kerner, Jr., who won election by a plurality of 524,000 votes. Moreover, Kennedy's vote in Chicago was acknowledged to be the result of an outpouring of his fellow Catholics, but— due to Carter's being a Southern Baptist and thought to be pro-abortion—many Chicago Catholics were opposed to Carter in 1976. In his final campaign trip to Chicago, in October, he had seen chilling evidence of this.

Carter got off poorly during this visit, after alighting from his campaign plane at Midway Airport on Sunday, October 10. He had been delighted by the cheers of about 2,000 persons, waving signs proclaiming their demands for a free Croatia, who had gathered to greet him; it was gratifying for Carter to observe this, President Ford having goofed in a recent remark about freedom existing amid Communist oppression in Eastern Europe. Yet, nagged by his hands-off stand on the Supreme Court's opinion on legalized abortion, it had to be disturbing for Carter to observe the clusters of right-to-life pickets, also carrying signs, who had gathered in demonstration against him. Then, still at Midway Airport, with Mayor Daley at his side, Carter goofed in off-the-cuff remarks, provoking titters that mystified him.

Using a campaign ploy that had won him applause in other parts of the nation, Carter started talking about the disruptive federal policy of creating superhighways that disadvantaged the poor, but not the rich. Obviously unaware that Midway was located near the heart of a corridor that Daley had marked out for construction of an exceedingly controversial billion-dollar expressway—apparently not briefed that Daley was proud of the superhighways that had been built in Chicago at his urging, slicing the city into so many isolated pieces of human pie—Carter said it was just terrible how these highways were being located in corridors that ripped into working-class neighborhoods, but never impinged upon the golf courses of the wealthy. His implication was that he would not tolerate this outrageously unfair practice when he took charge of things. Daley, wearing a sickly grin and visibly uncomfortable that Carter had unwittingly taken a shot at him, seemed relieved to put the candidate in his limousine and whisk him away, via the Stevenson expressway, bisecting many neighborhoods, to the inner city.

Daley temporarily disengaged himself from Carter when the candidate took off for a visit to the Tabernacle Baptist Church in Chicago's South Side ghetto. This was a fertile field for Carter to till and he was completely comfortable with the blacks, but it was not an area of choice for Daley to be on display; in mayoral elections they'd vote for him because they had no one else to vote for, but the blacks had not a trace of affection for their Irish Mayor. Reporters traveling with Carter could see that he was thoroughly enjoying himself in the church and that the congregation empathized with him; no one was going to marry his sister, but there was genuine understanding between these big-city blacks and the white peanut farmer from Plains, Georgia.

As those in the crowded church encouraged him with murmurs of approval as he spoke, Carter spoke of America's being the land of opportunity for all people and he played this congregation like a preacher as he closed his eyes and, with outstretched arms, talked of transforming the nation into a "beautiful mosaic of beautiful colors." Congressman Ralph Metcalfe, vocal enemy and political target of Mayor Daley, sat close to Carter. Carter had praised him and a grateful sound had swept through the church when he did so. Now, as the Southern white candidate painted word pictures of the brotherhood that he envisioned, Metcalfe nodded in solemn approval and wagged his gray-haired head from side to side. In the Tabernacle Baptist Church, Richard Daley might not amount to much, but Jimmy Carter was clearly "The Man." It was with gestures of reluctance that Carter took his leave.

The reception of Carter was not nearly so gratifying at his next engagement—the annual heritage dinner, in the Conrad Hilton Hotel, of the Polish American Congress.

Carter's staff people could sense a coolness toward the honoree as the 2,000 guests left the room where they had been having drinks to search out their tables in the Conrad Hilton's armory-like main dining room. The crowd was strangely reserved and not at all expectant or joyful. When Carter, Daley, and others who would be at the head table marched in, there was a scattering of applause—but hardly the ovation that might have been expected. A sullen attitude of reserve seemed to characterize the Poles who had gathered for this important dinner in, for Poles, their most densely populated city outside of Warsaw. It was as if the guests had a feeling of resentment about being there to honor Carter. It was as if a political bomb which might or might not explode had been hidden near the dais of this great dining room. A cleric boldly ignited the bomb.

A silence fell upon the vast audience as the Most Reverend Alfred Abramowicz, auxiliary bishop of the Catholic archdiocese, arose to give the invocation. The bishop prefaced his prayer by apologizing to his friends for being present. He had accepted the invitation, he said, before he knew that Carter had been invited. Carter cocked his head and measured the cleric.

Daley pursed his lips, rubbed his chin and, lowering his head, folded his hands in a gesture of resignation on his belly.

Abramowicz said that it had been with remorse that he had walked through a right-to-life picket line outside the Conrad Hilton, in coming in to the dinner. He said he had been urged not to attend. "I trust that no one misinterprets my presence here tonight." In a nonpartisan gesture, he took a slap at President Ford for his gaffe in saying during a televised debate with Carter that Poland was free of Soviet domination.

When he came around to blessing the food, the bishop invoked the help of God in behalf of "the people of Poland, who still bear the heavy yoke that checks their freedom." He cast a pall over the mammoth dining room, however, his point shockingly clear, when he lamented that the legalized abortion clinics of the United States were the equivalent of the Nazi gas chambers of World War II. Carter was unsmiling as he raised his head at the conclusion of this unique invocation. Daley appeared stunned. Moments later, bouncing to his feet after he had matter-of-factly been introduced, Daley launched a counterattack.

Speaking with some defiance, his head turned toward Abramowicz, Daley said, "Bishop, I don't think you have to be worrying about Carter, because he said, years ago, he's against abortion and he still says it and I believe him when he says it." Daley then said, "And I want you and all of these fine people, the fine Polish people at this fine dinner, to know that as the Mayor of this great city, I am one hundred percent for a free Poland." Then, thrusting his jaw, he added, "And I am also for a free Ireland." The crowd politely applauded.

When, eventually, Carter was called upon to speak, he avoided reference to the abortion controversy, speaking almost exclusively to the issue of freedom for the peoples of Eastern Europe. Carter praised Poland's heritage as a freedom-seeking nation; he ticked off the names of many notables of Polish birth or ancestry; he smiled broadly and said, "My daughter-in-law, Caron, is from Pulaski County, Georgia." The audience responded nicely to all of this. But the crowd apparently was disappointed when Carter merely deplored the refusal of the Communist countries to honor the human-rights provisions of the 1975 Helsinki accord on European security; the members of the Polish American Congress were better informed than Carter was, possibly, on the matter of the Communists' ignoring the guarantee of human rights that thirty-five signatory nations, including the Communist ones, had pledged to uphold. It was simply not enough for Carter to acknowledge that he was aware of grave promises broken; they wanted to hear something more aggressive than this from the man who wanted their votes for president.

As if to work up some enthusiasm for Carter, Mayor Daley started to applaud vigorously at two or three points during the candidate's talk, some of his faithful doing likewise, but the crowd did not take it up and Carter, taking no notice of Daley and his claque, continued talking in his Southern-preacher monotone. Finally, relaxing into a broad smile now, Carter expressed his thanks for being invited to the dinner and sat down.

Daley jumped to his feet, applauding. "Great speech, Jimmy, great speech!" But most of those in attendance at the Polish American Congress dinner didn't seem to think so; most of them were already heading for the exits with not so much as a backward glance at the candidate. Carter was observed in a wistful smile at Daley; this, clearly, had not been one of Jimmy Carter's most gratifying stops on the campaign trail.

Carter had come to Chicago to shore up his strength with the racial and ethnic blocs, the big election in which the outcome in Illinois might play so vital a part being now only three weeks away. In the course of two tedious days of campaigning in Chicago, it was Carter's intention to connect with every nonwhite and hyphenated-American group—and he nearly succeeded in doing so; as F. Richard Ciccone reported in the *Chicago Tribune,* the only ones he seemed to miss were the Chinese and the Irish.

Immediately following the Polish American Congress dinner, for example, Carter and Daley had scurried into another dining room to speak at a Greek-American dinner. Carter had been at pains, during his talk to the Poles, to make sympathetic reference to the fight for freedom in Romania, Hungary, Lithuania, and Czechoslovakia. To the Greeks, Carter said, "When we talk about majority rule in Africa, I don't want to forget about the deprivation of majority rule in Cyprus." From the look on Da-ley's face at these various appearances that Carter made, it was obvious that he was glad to be out campaigning, by God, with a man so dedicated to the cause of political freedom.

On Monday, October 11, Jimmy Carter walked into a private dining room of the Palmer House at 8 A.M. for an off-the-record interrogation by publisher Marshall Field IV and his minions of the *Sun-Times* and *Chicago Daily News.* (Daley skipped this.) At 9:30 with his wife, Rosalynn, and nine-year-old daughter, Amy, Carter attended mass at Our Lady of Pompeii Church— out on the Near West Side of Chicago, in a neighborhood that had been known during the shoot-'em-up Prohibition-era days as the Valley. (Daley didn't skip this.) October 11 being Colum-bus Day, the Italians and Sicilians were out to show the Irish that St. Patrick was not the only patron who counted in Chi-cago; consequently, every Italian-American politician of any consequence was there to pray with Jimmy Carter—including Congressman Peter W. Rodino, Jr. (D., N.J.), who had flown in for the occasion, and Alderman Vito Marzullo, dean of the Chi-cago City Council (having been a ward boss for the entire twenty-one years that Daley had been Mayor).

Jimmy Carter was driven directly from the Italian church back to the Palmer House, to meet with members of the Cook County Democratic Central Committee, Richard J. Daley, chair-man. Flanked by state chairman Jack Touhy and Daley, with Mike Howlett standing at Daley's side, Carter was enthusiasti-cally greeted by the nation's most tightly knit politicians—who wouldn't have given him directions to the men's room a few short months before. All of the state and county candidates were present, most of them hoping that now at last the presidential candidate would do something for them.

What the candidates wanted from Carter was his acknowledg-ment that he realized that they, also, were on the team and that he was personally committed to getting them elected, along with himself. There was a fumbling introduction by chairman Daley, in which he asserted that Catholic Chicago owed something to

Jimmy Carter. "Georgia," he said, "delivered for Al Smith in 1960!—no, Kennedy; John F. Kennedy, Georgia did, in 1960." Then the presidential candidate praised Daley for his record in consistently delivering the vote on election day and made sort of an apology to Daley for his having been kicked out of the 1972 Convention (this was the result, Carter said, of "fumbles" and "flaws" in the Democratic party rules). As always, Daley appeared pleased at the effort Carter made to be solicitous over the indignities that he had suffered at the hands of the crowd supporting Senator George McGovern at the 1972 Convention in Miami Beach.

Daley was attentive as Carter spoke of how grateful he was that Daley had come to his rescue after the Ohio primary, helping him to pin down the delegate votes he needed to clinch the 1976 nomination. There was not a sign of disbelief on the faces of the Daley people, although they were aware to a man that, after Carter's victory in Ohio, Daley had been in the position of having to hustle to get aboard a victory train that was about to leave him behind. Daley continued to keep his eyes fixed upon Jimmy Carter, as the candidate proceeded to lecture the tough old Democrats of Cook County on the evils of Watergate, the CIA, and the FBI—with Carter unaware that, in the judgment of these Cook County politicians, the only terrible thing about Watergate and so on was that somebody had tried getting away with something and had been caught.

Finally, in a moralizing tone of voice, Carter summed up his case: "The problem is not," he declared, "that the people don't trust good government. The problem is that the leaders haven't trusted the people." Then he stopped and there was applause, some of the Democrats putting fingers in their mouths to emit sharp whistles. Then Carter was on his way. As he walked out, smiling and waving, a ward committeeman grimly observed, "The problem is we are tryin' to elect a governor and that Georgia sonofabitch didn't mention Howlett even once. Not one goddamn time!"

Daley's mute acceptance of Carter's studied rejection of Howlett and the other Illinois candidates had not escaped notice of the Cook County Democrats; nor had it occasioned surprise.

They were accustomed by now to the fact that, while Daley was supposedly hopeful of electing his candidates, his overwhelming concern was to protect his own ass and no one else's. From straw polls that he had commissioned, Daley was quite aware that Howlett was lost. His information was that, with three weeks of the campaign remaining, Carter was leading Ford in Illinois by not more than an eyelash. Daley's worry was that the anti-Howlett vote would divert Democratic votes from Carter. If Carter lost Illinois, what kind of political boss would Daley then appear to be? Dear God, if the fellow got to be president without your helping him—how could you ask him to do something for you, when he didn't owe you anything?

Daley had felt smug at the success of his strategy in using the independent Mike Howlett to eliminate the recalcitrant Dan Walker in the March primary. That had been a coup, talking Howlett into giving up his almost certain reelection as secretary of state. Howlett's personal high standing with the voters, plus the heavy machine vote in Chicago that Daley delivered, had proved to be unbeatable.

It had been too bad, perhaps, that Walker had slashed and kicked poor Mike right up until primary day, leaking to the press the humiliating report that Howlett was tainted by a conflict of interest that put $15,000 a year from his former employer in his bank account. "I knew all about it," Daley had informed his inner council, and this was true because Howlett had told him. It was, alas, likewise true that when Walker was savaging Mike's bandwagon, damaging it to such a degree that hardly anyone believed it could be held together long enough to carry Howlett to victory in November, Daley had remained mute.

If Howlett had been so reckless as to continue accepting a stipend from his former employer, he could damned well get out of it as best he could; it wasn't Daley's problem—even though it had been Daley's judgment that Mike had done nothing to be ashamed of and even though Howlett had declared this outside income in the ethics statement that he had been required as secretary of state to make. What galled the tail off Daley was that first Walker and then Thompson had turned their guns of scorn on Richard J. Daley.

Quick to be angry when he was under attack, Daley was seething when Jim Thompson, the man who had put Judge Kerner and Tom Keane and, oh, so many other Daley men in prison, pounded away at him personally. Daley was furious at the newspapers for reporting Thompson's restatements of the Walker theme that Howlett was merely Daley's stooge and that, if elected, it would be Daley and not Howlett who would run the state. Increasingly, Daley couldn't resist striking back that Thompson was the Nixon Administration's hired gun. "Why don't they put that on the newspaper and on the television?" he cried. Daley's angry replies to Thompson, his accusations, were in fact thoroughly reported by the media, although Daley declared, "You don't find it, the honest-to-God truth, in the newspapers or on the television. Only the violence and the sex. Glorifying it, the violence and the sex!" At every opportunity, Daley lashed at the media.

In mid-October, about 500 editors and executives of newspapers located in twenty-six states, Canada, and Bermuda—as they gathered in Chicago's Drake Hotel for a three-day meeting of the Inland Daily Press Association—were astonished when the so-called greatest Mayor of the nation stepped up to a lectern and bullied them. Many of the newspaper people, getting their first look at Daley, were bewildered as he stumbled through a litany of castigation that obviously had been written according to his specifications.

He chided the newspapers for "creating a blanket image of every government worker as a payroller and every politician as corrupt." He sneered that the newspapers, aping television, had abandoned their role of "presenting all the facts," surrendering precious space to feature stories and opinionated commentaries, flooding the minds of the American people with gamy accounts of crime and sex. Red of face and with fractured phrasing, pushing his eyeglasses firmly onto the bridge of his nose, Daley regurgitated the warning of Wes Gallagher, retiring general manager of the Associated Press: "The First Amendment is not a hunting license."

Citing no source, Daley taunted the newspaper people that, during National Newspaper Week, just concluded, "there was a theme of genuine concern about the declining credibility of the press and growing skepticism of the press." Then, grimly, the Mayor reminded his audience of their own reports that an estimated seventy million eligible voters would shun the polls on November 2, two weeks hence. In true Bridgeport style, where it is sufficient to make an accusation without bothering to document it, Daley pulled his eyes up from his text, gave his listeners a defiant look and said, "You know and I know that the actions of the press itself have a lot of the responsibility."

This had been the kind of speech that exhilarated Daley, going into the enemy's camp and lashing out. He was, in fact, echoing a text that the born-again Carter was preaching simultaneously, in Tampa, Florida, that same night, Carter being sharply critical of voter apathy. But whereas Daley had been politely applauded when he concluded his scolding of the Inland Press people, Carter had been drowned out by boos before he was able to conclude his speech in Tampa. Pleased as he might have been by the generous space the Chicago newspapers allotted to reports of his remarks to the newspaper people, Daley had reason to be distressed by the companion stories from Florida, reflecting the poor reception that Carter had received in Tampa. In a brief meeting with Howlett, Daley complained, "They don't tell the truth, the newspapers, on Carter. All they try to do is try to hurt him, Carter."

However valid Howlett's doubts about Daley's interest in him might have been, Daley suddenly started working aggressively for Howlett as the November 2 election neared. Admittedly, it was far too late to reverse the landslide that was crashing down on Howlett and there was a heavy vein of self-interest in Daley's tongue-lashing of Howlett's critics. Yet, in speaking to a national meeting of United Auto Workers regional leaders, Daley became so angry he could hardly articulate.

"They keep sayin' in the press, the people are apathetic. Well, who is it that makes 'em apathetic? Who is responsible for this terrible thing, convincing the people they shouldn't vote, especially the young people who have been filled up with the violence, the crime, and the sex, only to sell the newspapers? I don't mind the adversaries or the disclosures, the dishonesty, but they depict every person who works for the city as a payroller and who depicts every politician like they are corrupt."

Turning then to Howlett, who sat at his side, Daley shouted, "They depict everything about this man on my left as bad, attacking him and his family, and he's a good husband and a good father, as you all know— And they attack him because of his association with me. What have they got, attackin' him, and why are they forgetting his great record of public service? Because it's his association with me! Listen, and I'll tell you something, I've spent twenty years in office and they would all like to get something on me, and I have a great record and all of the great service to the people of our great city and I haven't got a goddamn bit of apology for it." The UAW bosses thunderously cheered him.

A few days later, in an utter turnabout of style, employing now the soft Irish tones that he reserved for solemn occasions— speaking so quietly that his audience had to strain to hear what he was saying—Daley presided in City Hall at the annual awards program of his Chicago Beautiful committee. He spoke of the sublime mystery of flowers. "It is wonderful," he said, "to have the grandchildren sitting around and you tell them how a flower grows. You tell them how you plant the seed in the dirt and you tell them what will happen, about the sunshine and the rain, and how you can see it grow, the seed, into this beautiful flower—" Then, with patriarchal assurance, Daley said, "As we all know, the place closest to God is in the garden." One of the City Hall reporters unfortunately chuckled and Daley glared at him, the spell he had been weaving now broken.

In a final pre-election meeting of his precinct workers, Daley had another disconcerting experience. All had gone according to the usual formula—a band had played "When Irish Eyes Are Smiling" and "Happy Days Are Here Again!"; the candidates had made the customary go-get-'em talks. Even the ward bosses took a taste of the ham and yams that Daley provided; the man himself was introduced by some fellow running for Appellate Court judge as "the greatest mayor Chicago ever had, the greatest elected official in America"; and Daley himself appeared full of urine and vinegar as he made his final exhortation for a big vote, a few days hence.

Daley praised Carter. He sneered at the newspaper polls that showed Howlett was gone and that Carter was fighting for victory in Illinois, having slipped badly. Daley shouted in harsh tones that the press had been "full of falsehoods and misleading editorials, as well as lies." He made another effort to refute the indictment that he would strong-arm Mike Howlett. His gaze falling suddenly on Senator Adlai E. Stevenson, he thundered, "The Senator—you can ask him. His father—I never asked him for one thing as the governor, and Mike Howlett, as the governor, I'll never ask him for one thing, except to help the people of Illinois and help the people of Chicago." Few remembered that Governor Stevenson was out of office before Daley came to power in 1955 and that Daley had never been in a position to ask him for anything.

It didn't matter; the organization people were getting numb from the relentless pounding on the theme that the media and the Republicans were joined in an evil coalition to discredit Daley's good name. Even when he shouted, "As you all know, as everyone knows, I never asked a pound of flesh from anyone I supported!"—there had been only automatic applause. A woman in the crowd was heard to murmur, "I can't take this anymore," and she got up and walked out, Daley following her with his eyes, as if wanting to know where in hell she was going.

Others in the crowd then started to get up and sneak out, and a look of dismay appeared on Daley's face. It was unprecedented for the Democratic workers to walk out on a final preelection luncheon of this kind, with many speakers yet to be heard and Daley scheduled to make a closing demand that they do all things possible to get out the vote. Almost in despair, Daley jumped to his feet as the crowd steadily thinned out and shouted, "The ones who are leaving—don't be surprised to read in the paper about all the empty tables and how nobody was here." And a cloud of imminent defeat settled over the room.

On the last weekend of October, a few days prior to the election of Tuesday, November 2, the Chicago newspapers made a small retreat from their harsh criticism of Mike Howlett. Final tabulations of both the *Chicago Tribune* and the *Chicago Sun-Times* polls reflected almost a two-to-one voter preference for Thompson over Howlett. This was an unbelievable margin and there was agonizing at both newspapers over what the percentage of error might be; what was the profit of trumpeting a straw poll that might prove to be embarrassingly inaccurate? Thompson was crowing that he would defeat Howlett by more than a million votes. Howlett and Daley were stoutly insisting that the polls were wrong, Daley declaring, "They forget 1948, when they told us it would be Dewey over Truman; they aren't the word of God, the newspaper polls."

From his own poll of voter preferences, Daley knew that Howlett was down the tube, just as Howlett was reconciled to this from his own polling. Even so, the game requires that you kick and scratch to the very last minute, if only to protect others on your ticket who might have a chance of winning. Most of the polls gave Carter a fraction of a lead over Ford and this was the contest of highest priority in Daley's mind; it was imperative for Daley to put on a brave front, if he was to carry Illinois for Carter.

Carter's chances were improved by the pre-election newspaper reports that a softening of the voters' critical attitude toward Howlett had been detected, together with a lessening of enthusiasm for Thompson. Thirteen percent of the voters, the *Tribune* said, were undecided and while most of these voters considered Thompson to be more qualified than Howlett, "they generally feel warmer toward Howlett than Thompson." In the same report, the *Tribune* said that, while Howlett had previously been unable to project himself as being more than an extension of Mayor Daley's political power, he was now establishing his own identity and personal appeal with Illinois voters. The *Tribune* affirmed, however, that Howlett had little chance for victory.

Daley spent most of election day in his inner office of party headquarters in the Bismarck Hotel. Howlett, keeping out of sight in a suite at the Bismarck, talked to Daley two or three times during the day. "I told him that some of the fellows Downstate, the county chairmen, had called in to say they were getting a bigger turnout than expected. There wasn't any way of telling what this meant, but Daley said, 'That's good. That's good.' He said, 'It means they are voting for Carter and that is helping you.' Of course, this was bullshit; Daley didn't know any more than I did what a big turnout Downstate might mean. He was worried about carrying for Carter, you know. Not in Chicago; hell, he carried for McGovern and Humphrey in Chicago. Downstate, he was worried.

"The new people, Carter's, were running it Downstate and they didn't know too much about elections. That's why Daley kept hedging his bet, telling the people close to Jimmy Carter that his responsibility was Chicago and that they would have to take care of everywhere else in the state.

"That was Daley's way; don't take the blame for anything that happened outside of Chicago. But if Carter carried Illinois, then he would take the credit for it; you had to know Daley to know that this was how he operated. Daley never lost an election, to hear him explain it; other people lost elections. If you won, well, he would let you know that you couldn't have done it without him—and this was true, if the Chicago vote was big enough to put you over. But if you lost, even when the Chicago vote was not too hot—well, he'd let you know that this was your fault, not his."

Howlett would admit that—when the polls closed in Illinois on November 2, 1976, and the first Chicago precincts reported big pluralities for him—he had a surge of hope. Ward committeemen who had good news were quick to pass on the news to Howlett. Howlett's hopes were just as quickly dashed, however, by first returns from the suburban areas of Cook County and Downstate. "We could see, he was killing me, Thompson was. It was no news to me that I would lose, but I was shocked to see how bad I was getting hurt outside of Chicago."

Early in the evening, Howlett called Daley. "I guess I'm gone," he reported. "Daley said, 'It don't look too good, but you hang on and we'll see.' There was nothing, really, that I had to hang on to, but he was afraid, I guess, that I would concede and that our people would walk out of the polling places before the count was finished Downstate—leaving the Republicans to juggle the count to suit themselves. Well, he didn't have to tell me what was at stake and why I had to keep quiet; *I* knew that, for Cry sakes. We could see that Thompson was beating me by a million, maybe more than that; but it was important not to make a concession, or it could hurt the other fellows on the state ticket and Ed Egan for state's attorney; they were entitled to a fair count."

By about 10 P.M., four hours after the polls had closed, Daley projected that he would carry Chicago for Carter by a plurality of some 450,000, not quite what he had hoped for, but close. At about the same hour, he took a call from Carter's people Downstate and was jubilant. The inexperienced Carter people Downstate had made a projection, based on available returns from most of the 101 counties outside of Cook, and they reported to Daley that Carter was running close to Ford. Their information was that, while Ford was projected to beat Carter, the margin would be only 100,000 votes. What this meant was that, even though a heavy vote for Ford was piling up in the Cook County precincts outside of Chicago, Daley's vote for Carter should be enough to put the twenty-six electoral votes of Illinois in Carter's column.

"I talked to Daley after he had got the call from the Carter people Downstate," Howlett said. "I had called to tell him that we had seen enough returns now to see that I was lost and that I was going to bed." Had Daley expressed any regrets over the beating that Howlett had taken? "No, he would never say anything like that. It just hadn't been in the cards and we had known that for a month, for longer than that. We should have seen it during the primary. All the polls that Walker had taken before the primary showed that while the people in Illinois respected Daley as Mayor of Chicago, he didn't have the same standing with them as a political boss and they didn't want Daley dictating in Illinois government. The attitude in many Downstate communities was that they had to teach Daley a lesson this time, that he can't take over the state—that he couldn't take over the Supreme Court, the way he tried, and that he couldn't take over the governor's office. All of this, plus the way that Walker had dirtied me up personally, gave us a terrible handicap that it was impossible to overcome.

"I'm not saying that Daley was to blame for me losing; we

would have lost, I think, even without that because we made some pretty big mistakes on our own. But being connected to Daley, on top of everything else—well, I didn't have a chance. Only, he would never admit that he was a handicap; he wasn't the kind of a man who could ever admit anything like that."

Daley had confided to Howlett, in their last phone call on election night, that the prospects for Carter were exceedingly good. "He told me about the information he had from the Downstate people. I was surprised that Carter was doing so well down there, but I was glad to see him winning. I felt that way as a Democrat, even though Carter had not treated me very good; Carter, you know, is a lot like Dick Daley when it comes to taking care of himself.

"If you'll check on it, you'll see that Carter wasn't doing any bragging Downstate about being a pal of Dick Daley. He was like Paul Powell, who died with the $800,000 in the shoe boxes; somebody asked Powell Downstate one time about his connection with Daley and Powell said, yeah, it was true, and that he'd jump out the window if Daley told him to—provided that Daley would hold his hand. That's how it was Downstate with Carter and Daley. It was Carter's strategy anywhere he went around the country to keep a distance between himself and anyone who could be considered to be a political boss; it didn't matter who it was, and that's how he was in staying away from Daley."

On election night, at an hour when he was getting desperate for electoral votes, Carter had placed a call to Daley. "He wanted to know how he was going to be in Illinois, really needing Illinois, and Daley—who had had the call from Carter's people Downstate—made a terrible mistake," Howlett said. "He told Carter that he would carry Illinois. He told Carter it would be close, but that he was going to give him an edge of 450,000 in Chicago and that this would get him by. At that hour of the night, winning in Illinois could have been the ball game.

"But then, after Carter had been told this by Daley, Daley gets another call from the Carter people Downstate. They told Daley this time that they had rechecked their figures and that they had made a mistake in their projection. Carter wasn't going to lose down there by a hundred thousand; it would be by *two* hundred thousand.

"Daley must have died, hearing that. It was too late to take back what he had told Carter; the mistake made Daley look like an asshole. When he finally lost in Illinois, Carter probably wondered what in hell was the matter with Dick Daley that he couldn't tell what was happening in his own state."

It was at 2 A.M., November 3, eight hours after the polls had closed, that Daley got up from his desk in his private office on the fifth floor of the Bismarck, put on his topcoat and hat, and went home. He was poker-faced when reporters surged toward him as he stepped out of an elevator at ground level. "I'll see you later in the day," he said. "I'll see you at City Hall, later." Experienced reporters knew that this was his custom; win or lose an important election, he invariably put off his critique of the outcome until he could freshen up and get a little sleep.

Media people nonetheless pursued Daley as he walked with his bodyguards to his limousine. Would he have run someone else for governor—Alan Dixon, maybe, the Downstater who had swept to victory as secretary of state—if he had the chance to do it over again? Dixon instead of Howlett? "You never look back; you look ahead," Daley replied. Was this the worst defeat he had suffered as party leader? "Like my father used to say, the good Lord never slams the door in your face without leaving a window open." Then he was in the car and heading home.

Daley had said, just before he escaped from the reporters, that his mother had always told him that tomorrow would be a better day. On the evidence of the whipping his candidates had taken, there would be ample opportunity for tomorrow to be a better day. He had lost every office he wanted to win.

• Ford had beaten Carter in Illinois by a plurality of 93,000. Daley had produced a plurality for Carter in Chicago of 410,000, but this was 40,000 less than the bare minimum that he had forecast, and the Chicago vote would have been dismal if the blacks had not turned out in all fifteen of the wards that they controlled with overwhelming percentages for their Plains, Georgia, messiah.

• Thompson had crushed Howlett with an unbelievable statewide plurality of 1,390,000, humiliating the Daley organization by winning in nineteen Chicago wards and running almost even with Howlett in several others.

• Republican State's Attorney Bernard Carey had run 190,000 votes ahead of Daley's man, Edward J. Egan, making the Daley machine vulnerable to four more years of investigation by the enemy.

• Circuit Court Judge Joseph A. Power, despite the very best efforts of his mentor, Dick Daley, became the second judge in Cook County history to be denied the 60-percent vote of approval that is required for retention.

"I felt sorry for Daley," Howlett said. "I was a big loser and nobody likes to take a beating like the one I took. But—well, in politics, you have to expect things like this. Anyway, I had had a chance to adjust to what was going to happen; during the campaign, I could see that I wasn't going to come close. But I was in good health and I figured that I had a future—in business, if no place else.

"With Daley, it was different. He was at the end of the rope. Everyone talked about him running again in 1979. He was the kind of guy who would be thinking about the next election for president and all of that. Only, if you ask me, he wasn't in too good a shape, physically, and he must have realized that he was getting old and he didn't think he could last. So here he was, losing everything in his last election and no real chance to come back. I felt sorry for him."

The print was hardly dry on the newspaper reports of the pasting that Daley had taken in the November 2 election before the editorial writers started sounding a dirge for Richard J. Daley. Typical of what was being said was a *Chicago Sun-Times* editorial: "For Daley: The end begins." The editorial pointed out that Daley, although not a candidate for office, had lost everything. Daley had lost his clout, the editorial said; the machine had gone stale. Hedging, the *Sun-Times* said: "This is not a political obituary for Richard J. Daley or his machine. You can wonder, however, if the organ notes are starting to be heard in the back of the chapel."

Political observers were eager to hear how Daley would try to rationalize his massive defeat. The wire services and national news magazines and the broadcasting networks were geared to cover the traditional postelection press conference.

For the first time in the two decades and more that Daley had faced reporters on the day after, to alibi or to gloat, on November 3, 1976, he held no press conference.

"We had this arrangement," Mike Howlett said, "to get together in the morning. That was how we had left it, in our last phone conversation during the night. So I called Democratic headquarters about 9:30 and they told me he wouldn't be in. I said, 'What do you mean, he won't be in?' But they didn't know anything, so I called Tom Donovan, who was always with Daley and knew everything that was going on. You know, with Daley, they would never let you know what was going on; everything had to be a secret with Daley. But Donovan told me Daley was already on his way to Florida. I don't know whether he was worn out or couldn't face anybody, reporters and the rest of us, and Donovan said he didn't know how long Daley would stay down there in Florida. But I checked it out with some people at O'Hare, who know who is coming in at the airport and who is going out, and it was true. He was gone."

Seven weeks later, Richard J. Daley was dead.

Chapter Six

"Since Almighty God has called our brother Richard from this life to Himself, we will now bring his body to be committed to the earth from which it was made."

—John Cardinal Cody

AT ABOUT NOONTIME ON TUESDAY, DECEMBER 21, a polished mahogany casket was wheeled out of the McKeon Funeral Home. An honor guard of four spanking policemen and firemen snapped to attention, saluted, then lifted the casket into a gray hearse.

With the hearse following a blue-and-white police squad car that traveled slowly, the Mars lights flashing, and a fire chief's car, Mars light flashing, three limousines bearing the Richard J. Daley family coming then, with an unmarked squad car at the rear, the cortege encircled but one block of Daley's Bridgeport and came to a halt in front of the Nativity of Our Lord Catholic Church.

There was white and yellow bunting, signifying hope, over the main entrance to the church. His Eminence, John Cardinal Cody, clad in white robes and wearing a white miter, was peering through a window of the center doors.

As the casket was being removed from the hearse, a dozen police officials in uniform dress, wearing white gloves, formed a lane of honor through which the body of the great Mayor would be carried up the steps. Cardinal Cody, looking solemn, his fin-

185

gers intertwined on his stomach, now stood outside the doors. In a moment, he would flick holy water on the casket and recite prayers of reception as the remains of Mayor Daley were carried inside.

It was in this ninety-seven-year-old church, under the vacant gaze of plaster saints—where Daley had been baptized, received his first Communion, been confirmed; where he had proudly wit-nessed the baptism of his seven children; where he had marched two of his three daughters down the center aisle into marriage—that he would now lie in state.

About 500 persons had gathered to witness the arrival of Da-ley's casket at the church, which had been decorated prior to his death with pots of red poinsettias, in anticipation of the joyful feast of Christmas.

The casket was placed at the foot of the altar, the upper half of the lid open. Daley lay in a dark blue suit, with white shirt and conservative blue necktie, a black rosary laced into his folded hands.

In the early hours of public visitation, the four Daley sons stood at one side of the casket, soberly shaking hands with each person who came up the aisle. John Patrick and William, partners in the controversial Daley & Daley Insurance company, were first. Next stood Michael, the number two son, a lawyer, who reputedly was the brightest of the lot and closest to the Mayor. State Senator Richard M. Daley, the eldest son, was next.

Mrs. Daley sat nearby with her three daughters: Patricia Thompson, divorced from a real estate lawyer named William P. Thompson who had disappeared from the Chicago scene follow-ing the breakup of the marriage; Mary Carol, wife of a physi-cian, Robert Vanecko; and unmarried Eleanor, a schoolteacher. For the most part, the Daley women were silent, leaving it to the boys to shake hands with those who filed in to pay their respects. When people murmured condolences to Mrs. Daley, she nodded her acknowledgment but rarely spoke. Mrs. Daley was red-eyed; a friend of the family was heard to say that she was all cried out, but she did not allow herself to weep in public.

Outside the church, vehicle traffic was restricted, only dignitaries being waved through by the uniformed policemen who manned the barricades. Politicians were allowed to drive close to the church, as were Chicago's leaders of business and industry, financiers, social-register people—few of these people ever having been in this working-people area of the city that is called Bridgeport. Daley's wake, of course, was the biggest happening in the city, and the obvious place for the wealthy and members of the upper crust to be seen.

The plan had been to keep the Nativity of Our Lord Church open that afternoon and the first few hours after dusk. People came pouring in from all parts of the city and the suburbs, however; and as the evening hours passed, it became obvious that visitation would have to continue all through the night if no one was to be turned away.

It became bitter cold as night fell, with a wind chill of four degrees below zero, but still there were long lines of people outside the church, patiently waiting to get a look at the dead Mayor.

Early in the evening, the Shannon Rovers, the kilted bagpipers whose cheerless sounds had wailed at the walls at many a Richard J. Daley affair, came marching up the center aisle of the church. The Rovers, half a hundred strong and led by Tommie Ryan, resolutely fingered their pipes. Then, at a pause, Tommie Ryan declaimed, "Men may come and men may go, but the name of Richard J. Daley will go on forever."

Sis Daley was visibly touched. "Tommie," she responded, "he loved you." As the Shannon Rovers started out of the church, to the slow, agonized beat of their drums, Mrs. Daley raised her head and called, "Tommie!" And Tommie Ryan came back to the side of the casket, with two pipers and two drummers, and they played the ancient and defiant Irish drinking song "Garryowen," which had been Mayor Daley's favorite.

> *Our hearts so stout have got us fame,*
> *For soon 'tis known from whence we came;*
> *Where'er we go they dread the name*
> *of Garryowen.*

Down in Plains, Georgia, President-elect Jimmy Carter had informed the news media that he would attend the final rites of Mayor Daley. United States Secret Service agents consequently had gone to the Nativity of Our Lord Church for a look around. Keeping a respectful distance from the casket, the agents made a security check, from vestibule to sacristy, from cellar to ceiling, from altar to organ loft. They checked all entrances and exits, all windows; they were observed peering into confessionals, as if weighing the possibility that here might be a place where an assassin could hide. It seemed bizarre that such precautions should be taken in a church where a man was being waked. Yet, how many times as mayor had Daley himself voiced warning to be on guard against those who plot violence?

It had been to Colonel Jack Reilly, Mayor Daley's one-eyed director of special events—parades, formal dinners for distinguished visitors, and other ceremonials—that the Secret Service had had to go for a list of those who had received tickets to attend Daley's funeral mass. It had been Reilly who decided who was worthy to be allowed into the church and who wasn't. Most of the tickets had been given to the high and the mighty who had helped out Daley in one way or another, or to influential people who had not been partial to him, but who had to be extended courtesies nonetheless. The Secret Service was relieved to discover that these were people who could quickly be identified and cleared in the security check.

The humorless Secret Service showed no reaction when informed that the Reverend Jesse Jackson, disciple of the late Reverend Dr. Martin Luther King, Jr., and national director of Operation PUSH, had been relegated to a seat in the congregation, rather than the sanctuary. Cardinal Cody's judgment was, "I think he belongs in the political category. He is more of a political personage than religious." Nor did it amuse the agents to hear that Bishop Louis Ford, whose church was located in the black ghetto one mile east of lily-white Bridgeport, was to be seated in the sanctuary, as sort of a reward for his boundless admiration for the late Mayor.

Secret Service agents remained throughout the night in the Bridgeport church as the seemingly endless queue of shivering mourners came in out of the cold and slowly moved toward the casket. Until five A.M., at least one of Daley's sons had been present at the bier to shake the hand of every person who came in for a quick glance at the dead Mayor. Finally, at five, looking rumpled and dead tired, Richie slipped out to freshen up at the Daley home, nearby.

Secret Service had decreed that, for security reasons, the church must be closed at 7 A.M. to allow for one final check of the premises. When the doors were closed at that hour, Chicagoans had been paying their respects for seventeen consecutive hours. This should have been enough commiseration for the family of any man. No one had kept count of how many had looked into the casket; the conservative guess was 25,000, each person presented with a memorial card bearing a picture of Mayor Daley on one side and a prayer on the other.

At 7 A.M., the Daley family walked from the family home to the church for a few final and private moments with the dead Mayor before the casket was closed. Then they went back home to await the funeral mass, which was to begin two and a half hours later.

As dawn broke over Daley's Bridgeport that day, hundreds of people had already gathered behind the barricades that had been set up to keep them at a safe distance from the dignitaries who would be arriving.

Numerous uniformed policemen were on station surrounding the church. Network television crews were setting up. A tweedy man, claiming to represent Telefez Eireann, several times said in a soft brogue to no one in particular, "Oh, this is a sad occasion." News media people from Washington and New York sought crumbs of information from Chicago reporters: how far was it to the church from Midway Airport, where Carter would be landing? What was the history of this area, this Bridgeport? The names of dignitaries who were expected to arrive were being freely exchanged.

Vice-President Nelson Rockefeller was flying in. So, also, were Vice-President-elect Walter Mondale; Secretary of Defense Donald Rumsfeld, Attorney General Edward Levi; and the Democratic national chairman, Robert Strauss. Senator George

McGovern of South Dakota, who had certainly had his differences with Daley, would be present. Senator Edward M. Kennedy of Massachusetts, alert to the relationship his family had had with Daley, had been quick to advise that he would be there. So, also, would R. Sargent Shriver, husband of Teddy's sister Eunice Kennedy and onetime president by Daley's appointment of the Chicago Board of Education—who had been McGovern's running mate in 1972 —

Many United States senators would be there, including Adlai E. Stevenson III and Charles H. Percy of Illinois; many members of Congress; governors of several states, including Governor-elect James R. Thompson of Illinois and his wife, Jayne; the mayors of such cities as Cleveland, Newark, Pittsburgh, Milwaukee —

There would be judges galore and numerous state and local officials. A block of pews had been marked off for members of the Chicago City Council, who would be arriving in a caravan of rented limousines —

Everyone of consequence would arrive in chauffeured cars: socialites; civic and religious leaders; chief executives of the *Chicago Tribune* and the Marshall Field newspapers, the *Sun-Times* and the *Daily News;* big names in show business —

A. Robert Abboud of the First National Bank and John Perkins of the Continental, who were on the hook for a total of $55 million—a loan of extraordinary nature that they had made to the city earlier in the year, when their friend, Mayor Daley, pleaded for help—they had tickets for the church—and possibly a special reason to mourn, having lent the $55 million on Daley's personal assurance that it would be repaid.

Like at a sporting event, uniformed Andy Frain ushers checked tickets at the door of the church. In tough Chicago style, even members of President-elect Carter's entourage who had no tickets were not allowed inside. Moreover, on orders from the Secret Service the entrance doors were kept bolted until 9 A.M., the mass scheduled to begin just half an hour later.

Everyone had to wait outside until the appointed hour. Illinois Governor Walker was turned back when he tried to get in early. Secretary of State Howlett got inside through a side entrance, with Mrs. Howlett, but only because he had come to the church from a hospital bed. Taking a seat in the empty church, Howlett smiled at Mrs. Howlett and said, "Thank God this is still a city where it helps to have a little clout." Having clout, but reluctant to use it, Jimmy Carter, who had arrived earlier than expected, sat patiently in his limousine for ten minutes until it was time for the doors to be opened.

A forlorn figure in the sea of notables was Jacob M. Arvey, whose political roots were six decades deep. It must have been with a special kind of sadness that this dapper eighty-one-year-old survivor of many Democratic party battles had flown up from Florida. It had been Arvey, more than any other man, who had made it possible for Daley to be elected chairman in 1953 and mayor in 1955—and yet, in all of his years, no one had treated him as cavalierly as Daley had. It had mystified the old-timers in politics that Daley had so pointedly upstaged Arvey, neglecting him, refusing to be gracious, much less grateful, to him. Not only had Daley been obstinate in refusing to show Arvey the courtesy that was due him for long years of service to the Democratic party; he had even talked openly of dumping Arvey as national committeeman.

It seemed extraordinary that an old man who had been badly used by Daley, for reasons that Daley did not bother to explain—a man who had been the personal victim of Daley's arrogance—would trouble himself to come a long distance to Daley's funeral. But why had all the others come—Carter, Rockefeller, and all the others? One of the national reporters who covered Daley's funeral, Haynes Johnson of the *Washington Post,* took a stab at explaining it.

"A prince of politics was gone and they were observing the ritual," he wrote. "To the nation, Mr. Daley was known as the stocky, florid, bellicose boss. An aroma of 'the deal' always surrounded him. Daley the string-puller, Daley the head of a machine that could elect presidents, one way or another — " Yet: "To be in Chicago for Richard Daley's funeral is to understand, in a way, what it was like in China when Chairman Mao died."

Reporters who had covered Chicago's Chairman Mao on a regular basis were chagrined that they could not get into the church for the funeral mass. Some appealed to the police commander in charge of outside security for a chance to sneak in, only to hear him reply, "Listen, I couldn't get my own mother in there." So often frustrated by Daley across the years, the City Hall reporters were annoyed that, in death, the Mayor had screwed them again.

Likewise screwed, but accustomed to it, were the foot soldiers, the precinct workers, of the 11th Ward Regular Democratic Organization, Richard J. Daley, chairman. Wearing black ribbons on which were inscribed the words *In Memoriam,* the precinct captains who had consistently delivered the biggest vote on election days of all the wards in the city, meekly gathered behind the barricades across the street from the church.

It did not matter who had been a friend or enemy of the Mayor; you needed only a claim of importance to have received a ticket from Jack Reilly. W. Clement Stone, the Kewpie-doll insurance magnate who had contributed $7 million to the Richard M. Nixon reelection committee, had received a ticket. Bonnie Swearingen, the ubiquitous wife of chairman John Swearingen of mighty Standard Oil of Indiana, had one.

Most of the pews in the church were occupied, when shortly before the funeral mass was to begin, the family arrived. Quietly, they went up the steps and entered the church, walking up the aisle to pews on the gospel side—the left front, facing the altar. Jimmy Carter stood in his pew on the opposite side. As Mrs. Daley paused, he took her hand and kissed her lightly on the cheek. Rockefeller, next to Carter, reached out and took her hand and kissed her on the cheek. Senator Kennedy came up to Mrs. Daley and embraced her.

Reilly had placed Dr. Eric Oldberg in a front pew. "I am not much for these long-drawn-out affairs," he later said, "but I had a good view of things. The other half of that pew was occupied, would you believe it, by the family of the undertaker. The women were all dressed in mink and stuff like that and I thought to myself, they must make a hell of a lot of money off those Irish people out there."

After pronouncement of the "Rest in peace" near the conclusion of the services, the chief celebrant of the mass stepped forward. He was a Dominican named Gilbert Graham, a longtime friend of the Daley family. At the request of the family, Father Graham said, there would be no eulogy. Dr. Oldberg later recalled, "You could feel a wave of relief go over the crowd in church when he said that. God, I have heard some of the worst eulogies! They get the stuff on the fellow who is dead out of *Who's Who* or some crap like that and it is just awful to sit in a church and listen to such drivel. But, actually, this Father Graham went on to give a eulogy and he was damned good, too."

The priest began by saying that it would not be in Mayor Daley's style to have a eulogy. "The quality of his life and his actions are enough of a eulogy. That is far more eloquent testimony for this man, as is the presence of our nation's leaders coming here—a tribute that is deeply appreciated." He then went on to say that Richard J. Daley was known everywhere as a man who loved power. "Many interpreted that as political power, but that was far down on the list of his priorities. He was a man who had great power to love and a great capacity for love.

"No man wanted less to die than Richard Daley; he had so much to live for. But no man had less fear of death, because of his faith in God.

"He was our best man, a very special man. May God rest this beautiful man's soul."

The priest then recited what he said was Daley's favorite prayer. Vice-President Rockefeller gazed at the priest with birdlike attention and President-elect Carter closed his eyes and bowed his head at the words of the docile Saint Francis: "Lord, make me the instrument of your peace. . . . "

Cardinal Cody attended to the final blessing of the casket. Returning to the sanctuary, the Cardinal prayed: "Almighty God, we give You praise and thanks for all the good things that have come to Your people through this man's untiring service.

"Since Almighty God has called our brother Richard from this life to Himself, we will now bring his body to be committed to the earth from which it was made."

After the casket had been carried out of the church, the family following, Jimmy Carter and Nelson Rockefeller stood side by side on the top step, bareheaded in the wind chill of eleven degrees below zero, as the funeral cortege was assembled. As the procession of seventeen cars slowly moved off, with two police squad cars in front and two unmarked tail cars at the rear, the politicians exchanged quick handshakes and headed for their limousines. Carter was going back to Plains, Rockefeller to Washington; the Democratic aldermen were in haste to get back to City Hall, to dicker for the dead Mayor's robes.

Richard J. Daley was buried near the graves of his mother and father in Holy Sepulchre Cemetery, in an eight-grave plot he had purchased in 1946 when his mother died. "Holy Sep," as it was called, was located in the suburb of Worth, in a township that consistently voted Republican but was a traditional burial ground of Chicago's South Side Irish—leading to a little joke that Worth Township "is no place for a Chicago Democrat to live, but a great place to be buried."

A crowd of perhaps 3,000 persons had waited outside the green metal gates of the cemetery for a glimpse of the Daley funeral procession, the gates having been kept closed to assure privacy. It had taken almost an hour for the slow-moving cortege to travel the ten miles from Bridgeport, including a brief halt that had been made in front of Daley's bungalow on South Lowe. Many of Daley's neighbors had stood on their front porches, some sadly waving and some weeping; others had pulled back the front parlor curtains for a last look of remembrance at a man who had played so large a part in the lives of many of them.

At Holy Sepulchre, a cold wind was snapping at the fringes of a purple canopy that had been erected over a rectangular hole that had been air-hammered out of the frozen ground. The family and a few close friends huddled to hear the prayers of committal. Most of the mourners wept and Daley's children sobbed as Cardinal Cody, in white and red vestments, blessed the casket for the last time and stepped away.

In a matter of minutes, the mourners were back in the limousines, leaving their loved one to be lowered into his grave. Within the hour, cemetery workers drove up in a truck and buried him, striking the canopy and covering the casket with earth.

The wind whipped flurries of snow across the bare rectangular scar beneath which the great Richard J. Daley would remain for eternity.

He had had a funeral to satisfy his highest hopes. He had been honored in death and acclaimed. But now his time had run and as the wind cried on this gray December day through the naked trees of this graveyard where he lay, it did not matter much that he had been a man of great power.

He had no control over whatever judgment might now be made of him, mortal or divine. Eternally alone, Richard Daley had reached the destiny of all men and was, in death, no worse nor any better than any other man.

Index